ARE

Practice Exam,

Multiple-Choice

Divisions

Second Edition

Larry A. Paul, AIA

Professional Publications, Inc.
Belmont, CA

Acquisitions Editor: Elizabeth Fisher
Technical Editor: Robert D. Troy, Architect
Production Editor: Lisa Rominger
Copy Editor: Jessica R. Whitney-Holden
Book Designer: Jennifer Pasqual Thuillier
Typesetters: Mary Christensson and Sylvia M. Osias
Illustrator: Jennifer Pasqual Thuillier
Proofreader: Mia Laurence
Cover Photo: David Bergeron
Cover Designer: Jennifer Pasqual Thuillier

ARE Practice Exam, Multiple-Choice Divisions
Second Edition

Printed in the United States of America

Professional Publications, Inc.
1250 Fifth Avenue, Belmont, CA 94002
(650) 593-9119
www.ppi2pass.com

Current printing of this edition: 1

Library of Congress Cataloging-in-Publication Data
Paul, Larry A., 1946–
    ARE practice exam, multiple-choice divisions / Larry A. Paul. --
2nd ed.
        p.   cm.
    Rev. ed. of: ARE practice exam, non-graphic divisions. c1994.
    Includes bibliographical references.
    ISBN 1-888577-28-2 (pbk.)
    1. Architecture--United States--Examinations--Study guides.
I. Paul, Larry A., 1946–   ARE practice exam, non-graphic divisions.
II. Title.
NA123.P38   1998
    720′.76--dc21   98-42593
                                                          CIP

Dedication

It has been said that architecture is the world's second oldest profession. It is certainly one of the noblest. To provide humanity with basic shelter from the elements while enriching the built environment around us and influencing the lives of its inhabitants is the basic raison d'être of most every architect.

Many people say that they have always wanted to be architects, but few will endure the discipline of the arts and sciences involved in doing so. Those who do follow a long and productive career, building both large and small projects that give form to our lives and fulfill our dreams. I am proud to be a part of this profession.

This book is dedicated to my loving family, whose understanding and devotion have given me all the great joys of life. And I would like to acknowledge and extend my gratitude to all the educators and practitioners with whom I have been associated for sharing the knowledge, skills, and wisdom that have helped me succeed in the architectural profession. This book is intended to help those embarking on their careers in architecture so that they may succeed as well.

Larry A. Paul

Contents

Introduction

The architect's career usually begins with a formal education in a school of architecture where only the basic principles can be taught in four to six years. This schooling is followed by an internship with a licensed architect to learn the practical side of the profession. This "nuts and bolts" phase helps an intern architect discover how real projects are developed, how real buildings are constructed, and how real business is practiced. Knowledge, ability, and continuing education are what make an architect a professional who is valuable to society.

Once a candidate has fulfilled the required education and internship requirements and wants to become a licensed architect, in most cases the final step is the Architect Registration Exam (ARE). Each individual state or jurisdiction, however, is responsible for its own licensing process and should be contacted to ascertain the exact requirements and procedures for taking the exam. A few jurisdictions allow a candidate to take the exam before fulfilling all the internship requirements, while others require a supplemental interview or oral exam before licensure. All member boards subscribe to the computer-based examination prepared by the National Council of Architectural Registration Boards (NCARB) and administered by the Chauncey Group International, NCARB's consultant.

The ARE is administered by NCARB in all fifty states, five other jurisdictions, and nine Canadian provinces. In combination with the Intern Development Program (IDP) developed by the American Institute of Architects (AIA), the test's uniformity facilitates the reciprocal licensing process. Reciprocity allows architects who may practice in various locations during their careers to easily become licensed in jurisdictions other than those in which they were originally licensed.

The purpose of the ARE is to test the entry-level competency of a candidate to practice architecture within the acceptable standards of the profession in order to protect the health, safety, and welfare of the public. The ARE is constantly being changed and updated. Questions for testing competency are formulated and revised continually. Currently NCARB uses a completely computerized exam, which has replaced the paper-and-pencil format used until 1997.

Since the exam covers such a wide range of subjects, it cannot test every detail of architectural practice. The exam concentrates on the kinds of knowledge, abilities, and skills that are typically required of an architect in practice. Knowledge in specific subject areas, the ability to make decisions, the ability to solve problems, and the ability to coordinate various activities are all tested in the exam.

The Exam

The ARE consists of nine divisions, administered separately at a network of computer-based testing stations throughout the United States and Canada. The candidate may take a single division, all nine, or any combination. Six divisions are multiple-choice examinations. Those divisions are:

- Pre-Design
- General Structures
- Lateral Forces
- Mechanical and Electrical Systems
- Materials and Methods
- Construction Documents and Services

Each of these divisions consists of a series of multiple-choice questions with four possible answers for each question. The questions utilize both written and graphic material to test your competency. Outside reference materials are not allowed. Any reference material needed to answer exam questions, such as codes, tables, drawings, specifications, and other background information will be provided at the test site within the computerized test information package. Scratch pads for note-taking will be provided by the proctor and must be returned after the exam. Each candidate will have an individual computer work station containing a calculator. Simple instructions about taking a computer-based exam will be given before the actual test.

Previous exams have based many of the questions in all divisions on a sample building. Information regarding the building, such as construction drawings, specifications, and other data, is included in the test information package, providing the candidate with a simulated situation that could be encountered in practice. Questions may be based specifically on the information supplied about this particular building, on your general knowledge of the subject matter, or on how you apply your knowledge of those facts to such a building.

Four types of multiple-choice questions, and variations of each, are used in the multiple-choice divisions of the ARE. For each question, you are given four possible answers from which to choose the correct one. Of the multiple choices given, none are so incorrect or improbable as to be easily eliminated on the first reading of the question. You use a mouse to point to the answer you select from the choices presented on the computer monitor. The answers can also be changed or marked for later review, and you can move from question to question.

The first type of question is based on either written, graphic, or photographic information. In its simplest form you will be asked to select one of the four possible answers given. However, some problems will require you to make calculations to determine the correct solution.

A second question type has a list of five items or statements, and the four possible answers will be combinations of those five choices. You may be asked to correctly rank the various choices in some order, or you may be asked which of the five choices is correct or incorrect. A variation on this type of multiple-choice question will provide you with two lists and require you to correctly match items from each of the lists.

A third type of question uses a list of key words or phrases upon which questions are based. The questions may ask for simple definitions, or pertain to written or graphic information provided. You may have to look at a drawing or diagram or read about a situation, and then select your answer from the list. Two or more choices in the list may be very similar or appear to be correct,

but you may select only one. Be sure to select the best answer.

A fourth type of question presents you with a written simulation of a situation that you might encounter in actual practice. Drawings, diagrams, photographs, forms, tables, or other data may also be provided. The question asks you to select the best answer from four options, which could be words, phrases, or statements, given the context of the situation presented by the simulation.

These multiple-choice questions are formatted for computer-based grading, but they often require more than the selection of an answer from memory or the process of elimination. You may have to integrate several facts or pieces of information, review drawings, analyze data supplied in the test information, and/or perform calculations to determine the correct answer from the choices given.

The other three divisions of the ARE are graphic examinations. These are:

- Site Planning
- Building Planning
- Building Technology

Each of these divisions consists of a series of vignettes designed to cover a broad range of subjects related to site and building design, such as laying out parking; using landscaping effectively; and creating a block diagram, schematic design, accessibility plan, and mechanical and electrical plan. The six vignettes in Site Planning and a mandatory break comprise a total overall time of five hours. Building Planning is allotted seven and one-half hours, broken into three vignettes with a mandatory break in between. Finally, Building Technology has six vignettes with two breaks (one mandatory and one optional), for an overall time of seven hours.

Each division is allotted a maximum amount of time for completion, ranging from 3 hours for Lateral Forces to 7 1/2 hours for Building Planning. These time limits include time for general instructions, a tutorial before the actual exam, and an evaluation after the last group of questions. Most candidates will not need the entire amount of time to complete the exam. There is also a time limit for each group of test questions within each multiple-choice division, ranging from 72 to 114 minutes. Limits for subsequent question groups, which may be needed depending on candidate performance, range from 26 to 42 minutes.

The computerized mastery test is a variable-length test, so that some candidates may take more or less time than others. As you answer the first group of questions, the computer will score your performance. If your score is obviously passing or failing, then you have completed the exam and no more questions will be given. If your performance is not clearly passing or failing, the computer will transmit another set of questions. Overall, some candidates may require up to four sets of questions for each division to enable the computer to adequately assess their performance.

Typically, the divisions are administered year-round at a network of computer-based testing centers. Candidates now have the opportunity to take an exam on any day and in any sequence that they choose. Each division of the ARE may be taken twice a year until passed. Taking only one division at a time allows candidates ample time to prepare and study for each exam and helps spread out the exam costs. You are advised to consult the Bulletin of Information that is sent out by the Chauncey Group approximately one month before the exam for more specific information on the exam and the testing procedures.

Preparing for the Exam

This sample examination is designed to help you prepare for the multiple-choice divisions of the ARE. This guide formulates typical questions likely to be encountered, tests your knowledge of the material, simulates the actual exam format, and provides answers to the questions with notes explaining how the solution was derived. A bibliography suggests further reading useful when preparing for the various divisions of the exam.

A sample examination guide such as this is naturally limited in the amount of material it can cover. The more sample questions you can be exposed to, the better prepared you will be for the actual exam. Review as many references as you can, including your previous course work and textbooks in school, to renew your understanding of the subject matter. The only sure method for succeeding, not only with the ARE but with your architectural career as well, is to be thoroughly knowledgeable of all phases of practice. You can attain this through a combination of a high-quality, formal education, internship with a practicing architect, and broad-based experience.

In preparing for the exam, don't overstudy any one portion. Instead of trying to become an expert in any one area of the exam, you should review the general concepts of all the divisions. For example, the exam may

have a general question about reinforced concrete design, but you may not be expected to do a complete, detailed design of a reinforced concrete beam connection.

Have a good working knowledge of the concepts before you learn the myriad of details. It is much better to understand the basic theories and ideas of structural connections than to painstakingly memorize the whole range of possible connection details and materials used. After you fully understand the concepts, the application of those concepts and details is much easier to learn and to apply during the exam.

Taking the Exam

Once your examination eligibility has been determined, your state board will notify NCARB of the exams required. The Chauncey Group will send you the Bulletin of Information, which will detail the procedure for scheduling the test, tell you about the test content, and give you instructions on how to take the computer-based exam and on how to receive the practice software for the tutorial. The exams may be taken at any Sylvan testing site in North America, regardless of which jurisdiction has approved you for examination.

Schedule your study and review so that you can stop a day or two before the exam itself. Rest, relax, and get a good night's sleep before each exam day. Because of the breadth of the ARE and the concentration required to take it, the examination is an arduous process.

To avoid problems with traffic or getting lost, allow yourself plenty of time to get to the test site. If you can arrive early, you will be able to select a seat with good lighting and away from distractions. Once seated, prepare yourself so you can begin the test as soon as you are allowed. An exam proctor will review the general rules and answer any questions about the rules before the exam begins.

Remember, you are not allowed to bring reference materials to the exam. All necessary codes, tables, drawings, specifications, and similar reference materials will be supplied at the testing site. There are, however, some items you will need to bring to make the examination process easier on yourself, such as:

- watch
- snacks
- aspirin
- tissue

As soon as the test begins, start the computer program and quickly review what is in the test information package. Depending on the division you are taking, the material will include contracts, drawings, specifications, building codes, zoning ordinances, tables, and similar data for you to use. Don't study this material at this time, just know what is included so that you can refer to it when a question requires you to use it.

Note how many questions are in the exam division and how much time is allotted, and develop a schedule to follow. Allow yourself some time at the end to double-check your answers, answer any questions that you may have skipped, and make sure that you have marked only one answer for each question.

When taking the exam, if you mark an answer you are not sure of, make a note to yourself. If you have enough time left at the end, you can then review the question one more time and recheck your answer. Usually, your first response is the best.

Some questions may seem too simple, easy, or obvious. Make sure you understand all aspects of the question before answering. There may be a special circumstance or some exception to a rule that would preclude the easy choice from being the correct answer.

When words such as "best," "usually," and "seldom" are used in a question, be aware that your judgment will be involved in responding. The answers may be very similar to one another and will require you to discern the subtle differences.

Absolute words such as "always," "never," and "completely" used in a question should alert you to some exception that could turn a true statement into a false one or vice versa.

If you find a question that you feel is defective, such as one with two correct answers, make the best choice you can. On occasion, defective questions have been found in the exam. When this happens, either the questions are not counted or all of the correct answers are credited.

Time Management

There are a couple of methods for managing your time when taking a multiple-choice exam.

The first method is to start at the first question and answer every question regardless of its difficulty. To do this, divide the exam time allotted by the number of questions to determine the "average" time for each question. Some questions will take less time, some more. If you cannot answer a particular question confidently in the average time allotted or a little more, make a note to yourself and go on to the next question. You can go back to these difficult questions at the end of the test if you have time.

The second method is to go through the test three times. The first time, read each question and answer the ones that you are sure of and that do not take any lengthy calculations or study of the information supplied. This will involve skipping some questions, so make sure you note the ones omitted and only mark the ones you are confident of by pointing with the mouse to the correct answer on the screen. When you mark the questions you are skipping, make a note to yourself whether they need a little more study or further calculation, or if they seem impossible and you may need to make a best-guess answer.

The second time through the test, answer the next easiest questions, the ones that require a bit more study and concentration, or easy calculations. You should be able to answer these questions confidently. Make sure you point to the correct answer on the screen for each corresponding question.

For the third and final time through the test, you will answer the remaining questions that either require the most study or calculation, or require you to make your best guess from the four answer choices.

This second method of three passes through the exam will clue you in to its difficulty and help you budget your time so you will be able to answer all the questions. Once you have answered a question, though, don't reread and reanswer it during the next pass or you will deviate from your schedule. Again, usually your first response (or guess) is your best response.

Whichever method you use, answer every question, even if it is a guess. You will lose credit for unanswered questions, but you will not be penalized for guessing.

Keep in mind when scheduling your time that you will need to refer to the various background information included with the test information. You don't have time to read through it completely, but you will need to refer to it to answer some of the questions.

Good luck!

Examination Directions

When you have completed your other methods of studying for the examination, the examination on the following pages should be taken in a closed-book, timed format. This sample exam is intended to simulate the actual content and format of the Architectural Registration Exam. The questions range in difficulty to reflect the nature of the questions you can expect to find in the actual exam. Some of the questions will be fact-based, others require you to make an educated guess, just like the real examination.

The correct answers with brief explanations are found on the pages following each examination so that you may grade yourself and understand the logic behind the questions and answers. To fully realize the value of this practice exam, do not look at the answers until you have finished answering all the questions. After you have completed and graded your practice exam, the areas in which you need further study will be apparent. You are encouraged to study further to strengthen those weaknesses.

Please note the following:

1. Do not use any reference material when taking this exam. It is a closed-book examination, just like the ARE.

2. Read all questions carefully to understand the intent of the problem. Review the multiple choices, decide which one correctly solves the problem, and mark it clearly on the answer sheet provided.

3. All questions should be answered; do not leave any blank. If you are not sure of an answer, make an educated guess.

4. Time is a real factor in this and the ARE, so try to answer each question as quickly as possible. Be sure to correctly mark the answer corresponding to each question.

5. If you finish quickly and time allows, review your answers for correctness. If you realize a mistake, change your answer, but do not do so arbitrarily.

6. After you have finished the entire examination and have reviewed your answers, study the section detailing the correct answers and their explanations.

Examination Answer Sheet
Pre-Design Division

DIRECTIONS: Read each question and its lettered answers carefully. When you have decided which answer is correct, blacken the corresponding space on this answer sheet. Allow 70 minutes to complete this division of the exam. After completing the exam, you may grade yourself. Complete answers and brief explanations are found on the pages following each division of the examination.

1 Ⓐ Ⓑ Ⓒ Ⓓ   18 Ⓐ Ⓑ Ⓒ Ⓓ   35 Ⓐ Ⓑ Ⓒ Ⓓ

2 Ⓐ Ⓑ Ⓒ Ⓓ   19 Ⓐ Ⓑ Ⓒ Ⓓ   36 Ⓐ Ⓑ Ⓒ Ⓓ

3 Ⓐ Ⓑ Ⓒ Ⓓ   20 Ⓐ Ⓑ Ⓒ Ⓓ   37 Ⓐ Ⓑ Ⓒ Ⓓ

4 Ⓐ Ⓑ Ⓒ Ⓓ   21 Ⓐ Ⓑ Ⓒ Ⓓ   38 Ⓐ Ⓑ Ⓒ Ⓓ

5 Ⓐ Ⓑ Ⓒ Ⓓ   22 Ⓐ Ⓑ Ⓒ Ⓓ   39 Ⓐ Ⓑ Ⓒ Ⓓ

6 Ⓐ Ⓑ Ⓒ Ⓓ   23 Ⓐ Ⓑ Ⓒ Ⓓ   40 Ⓐ Ⓑ Ⓒ Ⓓ

7 Ⓐ Ⓑ Ⓒ Ⓓ   24 Ⓐ Ⓑ Ⓒ Ⓓ   41 Ⓐ Ⓑ Ⓒ Ⓓ

8 Ⓐ Ⓑ Ⓒ Ⓓ   25 Ⓐ Ⓑ Ⓒ Ⓓ   42 Ⓐ Ⓑ Ⓒ Ⓓ

9 Ⓐ Ⓑ Ⓒ Ⓓ   26 Ⓐ Ⓑ Ⓒ Ⓓ   43 Ⓐ Ⓑ Ⓒ Ⓓ

10 Ⓐ Ⓑ Ⓒ Ⓓ   27 Ⓐ Ⓑ Ⓒ Ⓓ   44 Ⓐ Ⓑ Ⓒ Ⓓ

11 Ⓐ Ⓑ Ⓒ Ⓓ   28 Ⓐ Ⓑ Ⓒ Ⓓ   45 Ⓐ Ⓑ Ⓒ Ⓓ

12 Ⓐ Ⓑ Ⓒ Ⓓ   29 Ⓐ Ⓑ Ⓒ Ⓓ   46 Ⓐ Ⓑ Ⓒ Ⓓ

13 Ⓐ Ⓑ Ⓒ Ⓓ   30 Ⓐ Ⓑ Ⓒ Ⓓ   47 Ⓐ Ⓑ Ⓒ Ⓓ

14 Ⓐ Ⓑ Ⓒ Ⓓ   31 Ⓐ Ⓑ Ⓒ Ⓓ   48 Ⓐ Ⓑ Ⓒ Ⓓ

15 Ⓐ Ⓑ Ⓒ Ⓓ   32 Ⓐ Ⓑ Ⓒ Ⓓ   49 Ⓐ Ⓑ Ⓒ Ⓓ

16 Ⓐ Ⓑ Ⓒ Ⓓ   33 Ⓐ Ⓑ Ⓒ Ⓓ   50 Ⓐ Ⓑ Ⓒ Ⓓ

17 Ⓐ Ⓑ Ⓒ Ⓓ   34 Ⓐ Ⓑ Ⓒ Ⓓ

Examination Answer Sheet
General Structures Division

DIRECTIONS: Read each question and its lettered answers carefully. When you have decided which answer is correct, blacken the corresponding space on this answer sheet. Allow 80 minutes to complete this division of the exam. After completing the exam, you may grade yourself. Complete answers and brief explanations are found on the pages following each division of the examination.

1 Ⓐ Ⓑ Ⓒ Ⓓ	18 Ⓐ Ⓑ Ⓒ Ⓓ	35 Ⓐ Ⓑ Ⓒ Ⓓ
2 Ⓐ Ⓑ Ⓒ Ⓓ	19 Ⓐ Ⓑ Ⓒ Ⓓ	36 Ⓐ Ⓑ Ⓒ Ⓓ
3 Ⓐ Ⓑ Ⓒ Ⓓ	20 Ⓐ Ⓑ Ⓒ Ⓓ	37 Ⓐ Ⓑ Ⓒ Ⓓ
4 Ⓐ Ⓑ Ⓒ Ⓓ	21 Ⓐ Ⓑ Ⓒ Ⓓ	38 Ⓐ Ⓑ Ⓒ Ⓓ
5 Ⓐ Ⓑ Ⓒ Ⓓ	22 Ⓐ Ⓑ Ⓒ Ⓓ	39 Ⓐ Ⓑ Ⓒ Ⓓ
6 Ⓐ Ⓑ Ⓒ Ⓓ	23 Ⓐ Ⓑ Ⓒ Ⓓ	40 Ⓐ Ⓑ Ⓒ Ⓓ
7 Ⓐ Ⓑ Ⓒ Ⓓ	24 Ⓐ Ⓑ Ⓒ Ⓓ	41 Ⓐ Ⓑ Ⓒ Ⓓ
8 Ⓐ Ⓑ Ⓒ Ⓓ	25 Ⓐ Ⓑ Ⓒ Ⓓ	42 Ⓐ Ⓑ Ⓒ Ⓓ
9 Ⓐ Ⓑ Ⓒ Ⓓ	26 Ⓐ Ⓑ Ⓒ Ⓓ	43 Ⓐ Ⓑ Ⓒ Ⓓ
10 Ⓐ Ⓑ Ⓒ Ⓓ	27 Ⓐ Ⓑ Ⓒ Ⓓ	44 Ⓐ Ⓑ Ⓒ Ⓓ
11 Ⓐ Ⓑ Ⓒ Ⓓ	28 Ⓐ Ⓑ Ⓒ Ⓓ	45 Ⓐ Ⓑ Ⓒ Ⓓ
12 Ⓐ Ⓑ Ⓒ Ⓓ	29 Ⓐ Ⓑ Ⓒ Ⓓ	46 Ⓐ Ⓑ Ⓒ Ⓓ
13 Ⓐ Ⓑ Ⓒ Ⓓ	30 Ⓐ Ⓑ Ⓒ Ⓓ	47 Ⓐ Ⓑ Ⓒ Ⓓ
14 Ⓐ Ⓑ Ⓒ Ⓓ	31 Ⓐ Ⓑ Ⓒ Ⓓ	48 Ⓐ Ⓑ Ⓒ Ⓓ
15 Ⓐ Ⓑ Ⓒ Ⓓ	32 Ⓐ Ⓑ Ⓒ Ⓓ	49 Ⓐ Ⓑ Ⓒ Ⓓ
16 Ⓐ Ⓑ Ⓒ Ⓓ	33 Ⓐ Ⓑ Ⓒ Ⓓ	50 Ⓐ Ⓑ Ⓒ Ⓓ
17 Ⓐ Ⓑ Ⓒ Ⓓ	34 Ⓐ Ⓑ Ⓒ Ⓓ	

Examination Answer Sheet
Lateral Forces Division

DIRECTIONS: Read each question and its lettered answers carefully. When you have decided which answer is correct, blacken the corresponding space on this answer sheet. Allow 75 minutes to complete this division of the exam. After completing the exam, you may grade yourself. Complete answers and brief explanations are found on the pages following each division of the examination.

1 (A) (B) (C) (D)   18 (A) (B) (C) (D)   35 (A) (B) (C) (D)
2 (A) (B) (C) (D)   19 (A) (B) (C) (D)   36 (A) (B) (C) (D)
3 (A) (B) (C) (D)   20 (A) (B) (C) (D)   37 (A) (B) (C) (D)
4 (A) (B) (C) (D)   21 (A) (B) (C) (D)   38 (A) (B) (C) (D)
5 (A) (B) (C) (D)   22 (A) (B) (C) (D)   39 (A) (B) (C) (D)
6 (A) (B) (C) (D)   23 (A) (B) (C) (D)   40 (A) (B) (C) (D)
7 (A) (B) (C) (D)   24 (A) (B) (C) (D)   41 (A) (B) (C) (D)
8 (A) (B) (C) (D)   25 (A) (B) (C) (D)   42 (A) (B) (C) (D)
9 (A) (B) (C) (D)   26 (A) (B) (C) (D)   43 (A) (B) (C) (D)
10 (A) (B) (C) (D)   27 (A) (B) (C) (D)   44 (A) (B) (C) (D)
11 (A) (B) (C) (D)   28 (A) (B) (C) (D)   45 (A) (B) (C) (D)
12 (A) (B) (C) (D)   29 (A) (B) (C) (D)   46 (A) (B) (C) (D)
13 (A) (B) (C) (D)   30 (A) (B) (C) (D)   47 (A) (B) (C) (D)
14 (A) (B) (C) (D)   31 (A) (B) (C) (D)   48 (A) (B) (C) (D)
15 (A) (B) (C) (D)   32 (A) (B) (C) (D)   49 (A) (B) (C) (D)
16 (A) (B) (C) (D)   33 (A) (B) (C) (D)   50 (A) (B) (C) (D)
17 (A) (B) (C) (D)   34 (A) (B) (C) (D)

Examination Answer Sheet
Mechanical and Electrical Systems Division

DIRECTIONS: Read each question and its lettered answers carefully. When you have decided which answer is correct, blacken the corresponding space on this answer sheet. Allow 60 minutes to complete this division of the exam. After completing the exam, you may grade yourself. Complete answers and brief explanations are found on the pages following each division of the examination.

1 Ⓐ Ⓑ Ⓒ Ⓓ	18 Ⓐ Ⓑ Ⓒ Ⓓ	35 Ⓐ Ⓑ Ⓒ Ⓓ
2 Ⓐ Ⓑ Ⓒ Ⓓ	19 Ⓐ Ⓑ Ⓒ Ⓓ	36 Ⓐ Ⓑ Ⓒ Ⓓ
3 Ⓐ Ⓑ Ⓒ Ⓓ	20 Ⓐ Ⓑ Ⓒ Ⓓ	37 Ⓐ Ⓑ Ⓒ Ⓓ
4 Ⓐ Ⓑ Ⓒ Ⓓ	21 Ⓐ Ⓑ Ⓒ Ⓓ	38 Ⓐ Ⓑ Ⓒ Ⓓ
5 Ⓐ Ⓑ Ⓒ Ⓓ	22 Ⓐ Ⓑ Ⓒ Ⓓ	39 Ⓐ Ⓑ Ⓒ Ⓓ
6 Ⓐ Ⓑ Ⓒ Ⓓ	23 Ⓐ Ⓑ Ⓒ Ⓓ	40 Ⓐ Ⓑ Ⓒ Ⓓ
7 Ⓐ Ⓑ Ⓒ Ⓓ	24 Ⓐ Ⓑ Ⓒ Ⓓ	41 Ⓐ Ⓑ Ⓒ Ⓓ
8 Ⓐ Ⓑ Ⓒ Ⓓ	25 Ⓐ Ⓑ Ⓒ Ⓓ	42 Ⓐ Ⓑ Ⓒ Ⓓ
9 Ⓐ Ⓑ Ⓒ Ⓓ	26 Ⓐ Ⓑ Ⓒ Ⓓ	43 Ⓐ Ⓑ Ⓒ Ⓓ
10 Ⓐ Ⓑ Ⓒ Ⓓ	27 Ⓐ Ⓑ Ⓒ Ⓓ	44 Ⓐ Ⓑ Ⓒ Ⓓ
11 Ⓐ Ⓑ Ⓒ Ⓓ	28 Ⓐ Ⓑ Ⓒ Ⓓ	45 Ⓐ Ⓑ Ⓒ Ⓓ
12 Ⓐ Ⓑ Ⓒ Ⓓ	29 Ⓐ Ⓑ Ⓒ Ⓓ	46 Ⓐ Ⓑ Ⓒ Ⓓ
13 Ⓐ Ⓑ Ⓒ Ⓓ	30 Ⓐ Ⓑ Ⓒ Ⓓ	47 Ⓐ Ⓑ Ⓒ Ⓓ
14 Ⓐ Ⓑ Ⓒ Ⓓ	31 Ⓐ Ⓑ Ⓒ Ⓓ	48 Ⓐ Ⓑ Ⓒ Ⓓ
15 Ⓐ Ⓑ Ⓒ Ⓓ	32 Ⓐ Ⓑ Ⓒ Ⓓ	49 Ⓐ Ⓑ Ⓒ Ⓓ
16 Ⓐ Ⓑ Ⓒ Ⓓ	33 Ⓐ Ⓑ Ⓒ Ⓓ	50 Ⓐ Ⓑ Ⓒ Ⓓ
17 Ⓐ Ⓑ Ⓒ Ⓓ	34 Ⓐ Ⓑ Ⓒ Ⓓ	

Examination Answer Sheet
Materials and Methods Division

DIRECTIONS: Read each question and its lettered answers carefully. When you have decided which answer is correct, blacken the corresponding space on this answer sheet. Allow 60 minutes to complete this division of the exam. After completing the exam, you may grade yourself. Complete answers and brief explanations are found on the pages following each division of the examination.

1 (A) (B) (C) (D)	18 (A) (B) (C) (D)	35 (A) (B) (C) (D)
2 (A) (B) (C) (D)	19 (A) (B) (C) (D)	36 (A) (B) (C) (D)
3 (A) (B) (C) (D)	20 (A) (B) (C) (D)	37 (A) (B) (C) (D)
4 (A) (B) (C) (D)	21 (A) (B) (C) (D)	38 (A) (B) (C) (D)
5 (A) (B) (C) (D)	22 (A) (B) (C) (D)	39 (A) (B) (C) (D)
6 (A) (B) (C) (D)	23 (A) (B) (C) (D)	40 (A) (B) (C) (D)
7 (A) (B) (C) (D)	24 (A) (B) (C) (D)	41 (A) (B) (C) (D)
8 (A) (B) (C) (D)	25 (A) (B) (C) (D)	42 (A) (B) (C) (D)
9 (A) (B) (C) (D)	26 (A) (B) (C) (D)	43 (A) (B) (C) (D)
10 (A) (B) (C) (D)	27 (A) (B) (C) (D)	44 (A) (B) (C) (D)
11 (A) (B) (C) (D)	28 (A) (B) (C) (D)	45 (A) (B) (C) (D)
12 (A) (B) (C) (D)	29 (A) (B) (C) (D)	46 (A) (B) (C) (D)
13 (A) (B) (C) (D)	30 (A) (B) (C) (D)	47 (A) (B) (C) (D)
14 (A) (B) (C) (D)	31 (A) (B) (C) (D)	48 (A) (B) (C) (D)
15 (A) (B) (C) (D)	32 (A) (B) (C) (D)	49 (A) (B) (C) (D)
16 (A) (B) (C) (D)	33 (A) (B) (C) (D)	50 (A) (B) (C) (D)
17 (A) (B) (C) (D)	34 (A) (B) (C) (D)	

Examination Answer Sheet
Construction Documents and Services Division

DIRECTIONS: Read each question and its lettered answers carefully. When you have decided which answer is correct, blacken the corresponding space on this answer sheet. Allow 70 minutes to complete this division of the exam. After completing the exam, you may grade yourself. Complete answers and brief explanations are found on the pages following each division of the examination.

1 (A) (B) (C) (D)	18 (A) (B) (C) (D)	35 (A) (B) (C) (D)
2 (A) (B) (C) (D)	19 (A) (B) (C) (D)	36 (A) (B) (C) (D)
3 (A) (B) (C) (D)	20 (A) (B) (C) (D)	37 (A) (B) (C) (D)
4 (A) (B) (C) (D)	21 (A) (B) (C) (D)	38 (A) (B) (C) (D)
5 (A) (B) (C) (D)	22 (A) (B) (C) (D)	39 (A) (B) (C) (D)
6 (A) (B) (C) (D)	23 (A) (B) (C) (D)	40 (A) (B) (C) (D)
7 (A) (B) (C) (D)	24 (A) (B) (C) (D)	41 (A) (B) (C) (D)
8 (A) (B) (C) (D)	25 (A) (B) (C) (D)	42 (A) (B) (C) (D)
9 (A) (B) (C) (D)	26 (A) (B) (C) (D)	43 (A) (B) (C) (D)
10 (A) (B) (C) (D)	27 (A) (B) (C) (D)	44 (A) (B) (C) (D)
11 (A) (B) (C) (D)	28 (A) (B) (C) (D)	45 (A) (B) (C) (D)
12 (A) (B) (C) (D)	29 (A) (B) (C) (D)	46 (A) (B) (C) (D)
13 (A) (B) (C) (D)	30 (A) (B) (C) (D)	47 (A) (B) (C) (D)
14 (A) (B) (C) (D)	31 (A) (B) (C) (D)	48 (A) (B) (C) (D)
15 (A) (B) (C) (D)	32 (A) (B) (C) (D)	49 (A) (B) (C) (D)
16 (A) (B) (C) (D)	33 (A) (B) (C) (D)	50 (A) (B) (C) (D)
17 (A) (B) (C) (D)	34 (A) (B) (C) (D)	

Pre-Design Division

Sample Examination

1. What must an architect know about a building to determine if the code requires smokeproof enclosures for exiting?

    A. its type of construction
    B. its type of occupancy
    C. its total height
    D. its total floor area

2. During the programming phase, an architect receives certain information from the client. Which of the following facts is not necessary to analyze and synthesize with the program?

    A. The site is zoned for commercial/light industrial use.
    B. Sitework is budgeted for only five percent of total cost.
    C. Customer areas need to be separated from production areas.
    D. The building is to be steel-framed construction.

3. When an architect develops a program for a building, which of the following should be considered?

    I. the client's requirements
    II. the user's requirements
    III. the user's organization
    IV. the contractor's qualifications
    V. the financing

    A. III, IV, and V
    B. I, II, and III
    C. II, IV, and V
    D. I and III

4. Which of the following terms describes a legal restriction placed on a piece of land that is created by a private party?

    A. a conditional use
    B. an ordinance
    C. a deed restriction
    D. a variance

5. For the construction of a building, the critical path has been determined to be 240 days. If one of the paths requires 80 days, what is the value of that path's float?

    A. 0.33 days
    B. 2.0 days
    C. 160 days
    D. 320 days

6. What is the primary use for fast-track scheduling?

    A. to decrease the cost of construction
    B. to decrease the cost of professional services
    C. to avoid future cost increases
    D. to guarantee project costs prior to the start of building

7. What is the urban design layout in most American cities based on?

    A. the grid concept
    B. the linear concept
    C. the radial concept
    D. the cluster concept

8. Which is the strongest determinant of the amount of solar radiation on a site?

A. location
B. wind patterns
C. latitude
D. slope

9. A large municipality wishes to build an exhibition and convention center. Which location is most desirable?

A. near an airport
B. adjacent to public bus routes
C. convenient to busy pedestrian routes
D. in a satellite location apart from the urban core

10. A shopping center parking lot is designed for 1000 cars. If the parking is at 90 degrees, and the lot has standard driveways, aisles, and turnarounds, approximately how large an area is needed?

A. 7 acres
B. 9 acres
C. 10 acres
D. 12 acres

11. A speculative research-and-development building is proposed for a suburban location in an area that is, as yet, completely undeveloped raw land. What method should the architect use to establish the value of the site for the client?

A. the land residual method
B. the allocation method
C. the development method
D. the comparison method

12. A client has projected a total budget of $1.8 million. The cost to acquire the site is $600,000. Approximately how much money will be allocated for the actual construction contract?

A. $900 thousand
B. $1.0 million
C. $1.2 million
D. $2.4 million

13. In analyzing the environmental impacts on an outdoor public plaza in the central city, architectural design could least control which of the following?

A. air pollution
B. solar radiation
C. traffic noise
D. afternoon winds

14. Which statement regarding construction time is incorrect?

A. Construction time is calculated in five-day workweeks.
B. Construction time can be shortened by using the critical path method.
C. Construction time is usually longer than architectural production time.
D. Estimates of construction time are only educated guesses.

15. What is the best way to achieve effective mitigation of urban noise?

A. Eliminate private automobile traffic.
B. Provide water movement to mask the noise.
C. Provide a dense landscaped barrier.
D. Increase the distance between the source and the receiver.

16. Which of the following is the most important factor in determining whether a building design is considered formal?

A. symmetry
B. scale
C. proportion
D. form

17. A three-story building on a half-acre site has a floor plate of 10,000 square feet and an efficiency factor of 80 percent. What is the floor area ratio (FAR)?

A. 0.5
B. 0.9
C. 1.1
D. 1.4

18. A geotechnical survey has been requested for a client's site. Which of the following is not a factor in determining the number of test borings to be taken by the soils engineer?

A. the building footprint
B. the uniformity of subsurface conditions
C. the depth at which rock strata is found
D. the discovery of the ground water table

19. The schematic design of a 112,000 square foot speculative office building proposes a 75-percent efficiency factor. However, to make the project financially successful, the building developer requires the efficiency factor to be 80 percent. To satisfy the developer, how much additional net rentable area must the architect provide?

    A. 4480 square feet
    B. 5250 square feet
    C. 5600 square feet
    D. 7000 square feet

20. Which of the following would influence a design to restore and enlarge a Greek Revival building from the 1800s?

    A. the groins of the cross vaults
    B. the angle of the flying buttresses
    C. the radii of the pendentives
    D. the entasis of the columns

21. With which of the following is a government postal facility not required to comply?

    A. local regulations
    B. OSHA regulations
    C. ANSI standards
    D. EIR procedures

22. What is an aquifer?

    A. surface soil that is saturated by heavy rainfall runoff
    B. underground permeable material through which water flows
    C. the boundary between the saturation zone and the aeration zone
    D. the boundary between soil layers subject to seismic erosion

23. How do pier and grade beam foundations compare with conventional spread footings?

    A. They are more expensive.
    B. They are more easily constructed.
    C. They are more capable of supporting greater loads.
    D. They are are more permanent.

24. Flexibility is often an important program requirement in the architectural design of a building. Which of the following types require the least flexibility?

    A. school classrooms
    B. hospital patient rooms
    C. shopping center tenant spaces
    D. church social halls

25. The programming phase of an architectural project is which of the following processes?

    A. discovering the problems
    B. acknowledging the problems
    C. interpreting the problems
    D. resolving the problems

26. What is the primary reason that suburban shopping centers have replaced older shopping areas in downtown cores?

    A. People prefer to drive to shopping centers.
    B. The lack of public transit makes downtowns less accessible.
    C. Cities have been unable to control the increase in crime.
    D. High property taxes force retailers to other locations.

27. Which form of real estate ownership exists for a limited period of time?

    A. condominium
    B. fee simple
    C. leasehold
    D. conditional use

28. How are zoning requirements for front setbacks expressed?

    A. the distance between the front lot line and the building
    B. the distance between the sidewalk and the building front
    C. the distance between the centerline of the street and the building front
    D. a percentage of the lot depth

29. Which of the following do not directly impose legal constraints on the proposed development of land?

    A. deed restrictions
    B. easements
    C. zoning regulations
    D. Environmental Impact Reports

30. Which of the following issues is not relevant in the analysis of a particular site for proper building orientation?

    A. The building is to be heated by solar energy.
    B. Prevailing winds are from the northwest.
    C. A freeway to the east creates traffic noise.
    D. Neighboring buildings have pier and grade beam foundations.

31. In the site analysis for a proposed building, which of the following conditions would indicate the potential for poor site drainage?

    I. no storm drainage system
    II. relatively flat site
    III. existing dense groundcover
    IV. existing high water table
    V. existing flowing stream

    A. I, II, and IV
    B. III, IV, and V
    C. I and III
    D. I, III, and IV

32. At the conclusion of the programming phase of a building project, how should the space needs of the client be expressed?

    A. in terms of dimensions
    B. in terms of proportions
    C. in terms of areas
    D. in terms of configurations

33. Which of the following is not usually used as a standard basis for preliminary cost estimating of a project in the pre-design phase?

    A. cost per student
    B. cost per inmate
    C. cost per pedestrian
    D. cost per bed

34. An unoccupied office building is located within the limits of a city's redevelopment area. The city agency has offered the owner a price to purchase it, but the owner refuses to sell. Which of the following is true?

    A. The city must pay fair market value for the land but only salvage value for the vacant building.
    B. The city must pay the owner at least what the owner originally paid for the property.
    C. The owner is required by law to accept the price offered by the city.
    D. The city could take the property from the owner before the final price is determined.

35. Which of the following is not an intention of zoning ordinances?

    A. to minimize fire danger
    B. to restrict lot coverage
    C. to limit population density
    D. to segregate different uses

36. To produce a specific project in an architect's office, what do the staffing and scheduling requirements primarily depend upon?

    A. the project's quality
    B. the project's complexity
    C. the project's cost
    D. the project's size

37. What is the main objective of a building program?

    A. to discover the building's function and purpose
    B. to define the essential building problem
    C. to determine the schematic building solution
    D. to decide the prototypical building form

38. Many building types commonly use a 36-inch-wide doorway. How is this width generally established?

    A. by typical human dimensions
    B. by traditional use
    C. by building industry standards
    D. by code requirements

39. Which of the following factors will not lower the cost of a project?

    A. harmonious proportions
    B. regular forms
    C. compact arrangements
    D. high densities

40. When scheduling a project using the critical path method (CPM), if the critical path time is reduced, which of the following is likely?

    A. The project quality will not be affected.
    B. The float time will not be affected.
    C. The construction time will be extended.
    D. The project cost will be increased.

41. Building codes usually refer to both exit and means of egress. What is the definition of *means of egress*?

    A. the same as an exit
    B. the legal ways out of a building
    C. the emergency ways out of a building
    D. all the ways out of a building

42. Which of the following characteristics are employed by building codes to classify various building types and structures?

  I. construction type
  II. fire hazard
  III. occupancy group
  IV. land use

A. I, III, and IV
B. II, III, and IV
C. I, II, and III
D. I, II, and IV

43. In the pre-design phase, an architect estimates that an office building can be constructed for $90.00 per square foot at today's construction costs. The cost index used for that estimate is 1050. When the project is built one year from today, the cost index is projected to be 1260. What will be the estimated construction cost then?

A. $90.00 per square foot
B. $94.50 per square foot
C. $108.00 per square foot
D. $113.40 per square foot

44. The catchment area is the prime determinant for the size and type of a planned community shopping center. What is the definition of *catchment area*?

A. the area needed to site a major department store and its required parking
B. the area from which its user population comes
C. the area within a 30-minute driving radius of the center
D. the area containing a sufficient user population to make the center viable

45. Your client has purchased a 100,000-square-foot site. Zoning for the site allows a maximum FAR of 4.0. Half the site needs to be utilized for parking requirements. How many stories must the building design have to achieve the maximum size allowed?

A. 2 stories
B. 4 stories
C. 8 stories
D. 10 stories

46. What is the primary goal in designing good pedestrian circulation?

A. speed
B. safety
C. economy
D. permanence

47. To accommodate the handicapped, ANSI standards require that accessible routes must be which of the following?

  I. free of all protruding objects
  II. designed for all disabilities
  III. designed for all interior locations only
  IV. continuous
  V. unobstructed

A. II, IV, and V
B. I, II, and III
C. I, II, IV, and V
D. I and II

48. Zoning regulations for an office building require space for one car for every 300 square feet of occupied area. If the proposed building has 80,000 gross square feet and an efficiency factor of 0.8, how many acres of land should be planned to provide for the required parking?

A. 1.8 acres
B. 2.0 acres
C. 2.4 acres
D. 3.1 acres

49. If a particular building wall assembly has a high U-factor attached to it, where should it primarily be used?

A. in areas that have small daily temperature variations
B. in areas that have a constantly cold climate
C. in areas that have a moderate climate all year
D. in areas that have a constantly hot climate

50. As part of the initial program, the initial budget for the cost of construction provided by the architect is based on what?

A. the volume method
B. the unit cost method
C. historical costs of similar projects
D. the per-square-foot cost method

Examination Answers with Explanations

1. **C** Smokeproof enclosures for exiting are required by building codes when a structure exceeds a specific height regardless of occupancy, construction type, or floor area. The purpose of such enclosures is to allow building occupants to exit safely without encountering the hazard of rising smoke from a building fire.

2. **D** Essential to the programming process are collecting, organizing, and analyzing facts from the client and other sources. The architect must discriminate between those facts that are relevant and those that are unimportant at that stage. Among those facts listed, site zoning, project budget, and functional-spatial relationships are pertinent to programming. The type of construction framing is the kind of information to be considered at a later stage of project development, such as schematic design.

3. **B** In developing a program for a client, all of the factors related to the client and the users should be considered. The financing and contractor's qualifications, though important in the building process, do not directly bear on the program itself.

4. **C** Private parties may place conditions, covenants and/or restrictions for property in clauses known as deed restrictions. An ordinance is a law or regulation on property imposed by governmental authorities. Variances and conditional uses are specific approvals given by governmental authorities in special circumstances, for a property owner to do a particular action related to the property.

5. **C** The float is the difference in time between the critical path and any other path. Since this critical path was 240 days and the path in question was 80 days, the difference is 160 days. There are 160 days of additional time during the overall critical path for other activities to happen without delaying the completion of the project.

6. **C** Fast-track scheduling is the best method to decrease the time between starting and finishing construction of a project. Fast-tracking increases professional services and fees by requiring the preparation of separate bid packages for various phases of the project. These separate bid packages make it difficult to know the final cost of the project until construction is well underway, so it cannot reduce construction costs. It does reduce construction time, however, which avoids future cost increases due to inflation.

7. **A** The grid concept was predominantly used to lay out most American cities, from colonial times to present-day developers. Early towns were developed in large square blocks with a central common still in use today. The grid layout is a simple, understandable format for urban design, organization, and identity, that allows for ease of surveying and recording of parcels of land, and facilitates land development.

8. **D** The angle between the ground and the sun's rays is the primary determinant of how much solar radiation a site will receive. The more perpendicular the sun's position to the ground, the less reflection and the more direct radiation. Therefore, the slope of the ground relative to the sun is the correct answer.

9. **B** A major facility serving large numbers of people should be readily accessible by car or public transportation. Pedestrian routes are not nearly as important. A nearby airport would also not be a major consideration and may even cause noise problems. A satellite site, remote from the city center, would be lacking in services and adequate transportation to and from lodging facilities and other amenities.

10. **B** To calculate the area required for parking, the number of square feet allowed per car and the number of square feet in an acre must be known. Normally, 400 square feet per car allows for both the parking space and the circulation space. Therefore,

$$(1000) \text{ cars} \left(400 \, \frac{\text{ft}^2}{\text{car}}\right) = 400{,}000 \, \text{ft}^2$$

Dividing this number by the number of square feet per acre,

$$\frac{400{,}000 \, \text{ft}^2}{\dfrac{43{,}560 \, \text{ft}^2}{\text{acre}}} = 9.18 \, \text{acres}$$

9.0 is closest to the correct answer of 9.18 acres.

11. **C** The land allocation method is used for existing improved property to allocate value between the land and the improvements thereon. The residual method is used where no vacant land exists, such as in highly developed areas. The comparison method is appropriate where similarly developed property is being bought and sold, enabling values to be compared. Since in this case, sales prices of comparable land are nonexistent, the only reliable method for valuation of this property would be the development method which estimates the development costs of a parcel.

12. **B** First, the land cost of $600,000 is subtracted from the $1.8 million, leaving $1.2 million for the project construction budget. This amount is somewhat larger than the actual construction contract cost. The construction budget also includes land surveys, soils tests, professional fees, inspections and testing, furnishings, etc., which typically average 15 percent of the actual cost. Dividing $1.2 million by 1.15 (100 plus 15 percent) equals $1.04 million, which is closest to $1.0 million.

13. **A** Of all the environmental impacts listed, air pollution would be somewhat impossible to control through design. Solar radiation can be controlled by sunshades, overhangs, trellises, trees, etc. Traffic noise can be attenuated by solid barriers or masked by white noise generators such as music or running water. Afternoon wind can be effectively blocked by barriers or landscaping.

14. **B** Construction time is based upon the five-day workweek calculated in calendar days. It is also generally based on prior experience with similar types of projects and procedures and requires skillful judgment and educated guesswork. It is typically longer in duration than the production time for architectural drawings to be completed. The critical path method does not affect the actual construction time, though. CPM only allows for the planning and scheduling of a project to optimize the allocation of manpower and resources of the various operational tasks that take place. It also identifies the critical areas of control.

15. **D** Every city faces the problem of noise pollution and its control. Each method listed would provide some reduction and relief. Landscaping reflects the noise and disperses it, while moving water masks noise, making it less objectionable. Eliminating private cars would reduce the source of noise but other vehicular traffic from buses, trucks, emergency vehicles, etc., would still create problems. Since the level of sound is inversely related to the square of the distance between the source and the receiver, the most effective solution would be to increase this distance as much as possible to decrease the sound level reaching the receiver.

16. **A** Symmetry is the balanced arrangement of elements that are exactly the same relative to a center or axis. Throughout history, from ancient Egypt and Rome to present-day governmental buildings, the concept of formality has been strongly associated with symmetry. Since much in nature is relatively symmetrical, society has developed most of its man-made objects to be symmetrical as well.

17. **D** The solution to this problem lies in the understanding of the concept of floor area ratio (FAR). FAR is the ratio of the gross floor area of a building to the site area. The site area is one-half acre, so

$$\left(\frac{1}{2}\right)(43,560\,\text{ft}^2) = 21,780\,\text{ft}^2$$

The building's gross area is calculated by multiplying the number of stories by the area of each floor plate.

$$(3)(10,000\,\text{ft}^2) = 30,000\,\text{ft}^2$$

Therefore, the FAR is

$$\frac{30,000\,\text{ft}^2}{21,780\,\text{ft}^2} = 1.38$$

Round this to 1.4. The efficiency factor is unrelated to the floor area ratio.

18. **C** Geotechnical engineers utilize test borings drilled in various locations on a site to investigate subsoil conditions in order to make foundation recommendations. If subsurface conditions are relatively uniform, fewer borings need to be taken. If the building footprint is large or the shape complex, usually more borings are required to make proper foundation recommendations. Encountering ground water will require more borings to determine its extent and location. The depth of rock or firm strata underlying the surface will not affect the number of borings as the strata may vary across the site.

19. **C** Net rentable area divided by gross building area is the efficiency factor ratio. The original net area is calculated by multiplying the original efficiency by the gross area.

$$(0.75)(112,000\,\text{ft}^2) = 84,000\,\text{ft}^2$$

The new required net area would be

$$(0.80)(112,00\,\text{ft}^2) = 89,600\,\text{ft}^2$$

The difference would be

$$89,600\,\text{ft}^2 - 84,000\,\text{ft}^2 = 5600\,\text{ft}^2$$

Another way to solve the problem would be to multiply the gross area by the difference in efficiency factors.

$$0.80 - 0.75 = 0.05$$
$$(0.05)(112,000\,\text{ft}^2) = 5600\,\text{ft}^2$$

20. **D** The ancient Romans developed groins as the joints where two barrel vaults intersected at right angles. Gothic buildings used flying buttresses to structurally resist the outward forces created by their vaulted roofs on the side walls. In building circular domes over square spaces, the Byzantines created pendentives. The Greek architects devised the concept of entasis, the tapering of columns to visually correct an optical illusion. A Greek Revival building would have columns built with entasis, which would need to be considered in the restoration and the design of any addition to it.

21. **A** Local regulations are superseded by federal regulations for all state and federal building projects and need not be complied with. Government projects must comply with Occupational Safety and Health Act regulations, ANSI standards for the handicapped, and the requirement to file an Environmental Impact Report (EIR).

22. **B** Water flows through the permeable earth or rock underground known as an aquifer, which can be the source of water supply for a building project. The boundary between the zone of saturation and the zone of aeration defines the ground water table.

23. **A** Pier and grade foundations are used when the soil conditions near the surface are incapable of providing any real bearing values to support the building. They are generally more expensive than conventional spread footings, requiring pier drilling, more reinforcement, more concrete, and more labor due to their difficulty in forming, placing, and construction. They do not support any greater loads as either system is designed to carry whatever loads are imposed upon it. Since both systems utilize concrete construction, neither is more permanent than the other.

24. **B** In all of the types listed except hospital patient rooms, flexibility is an important design parameter. Because individual toilets need to be provided in each patient room, the location of those plumbing facilities eliminates the potential for flexibility. These plumbing requirements rigidly dictate room arrangement and preclude the possibility of easy changes.

25. **A** Programming is the process of problem seeking, or discovering the problems inherent in an architectural project. It identifies and clarifies owner/user goals, analyzes facts, and determines needs so that problems can be revealed and expressed. Once a program is developed, the problems can be acknowledged, with possible solutions interpreted and a final design established that resolves identified problems.

26. **B** As society grew more dependent on the private automobile, public transit systems became less viable. As residential development spread from the urban core to the suburbs, the automobile became a necessity because public transit failed to follow this development. Retail businesses were forced to relocate closer and more convenient to the public they served.

27. **C** Condominium ownership is a type of permanent ownership in a shared common property and is in perpetuity, albeit with covenants, conditions, and restrictions (CC&Rs). Fee simple is the most common form of property ownership whereby property is owned totally and outright in perpetuity. A conditional use is a right granted for a specific period of time and a specific use of a property by a local jurisdiction, but it carries no right of real estate ownership itself. A leasehold is a form of ownership in real estate for a limited period of time, that is, the length of the lease.

28. **A** Zoning regulations and ordinances govern such things as height, bulk, floor area ratio, density, parking, and setbacks to provide adequate light, air, and privacy and to reduce hazards from traffic, emergencies, and congestion. Setbacks are usually expressed as a number of fixed dimensions, measurements, and/or relationships. Setbacks are not related to sidewalks because the relationship of the sidewalk to the property boundaries is not absolute or certain. Percentages of lot dimensions are sometimes used to provide side or rear yard setbacks, but they are not used for front setbacks.

29. **D** Deed restrictions, easements, and zoning ordinances are all legal restrictions on the use and development of real estate. Environmental Impact Reports (EIRs) are only a means to assess the potential negative impact that a project may have on the environment and to study possible alternatives to mitigate those impacts. EIRs are used by regulatory agencies to review and approve or disapprove a project, but they are not legal constraints in and of themselves.

30. **D** External influences are the prime determinants of building orientation on a particular site. Consideration of climate, noise, and views plays a major role in the placement of a building to provide shelter from the weather, privacy, and insulation from noise sources. Also, proper orientation of building components is important when solar energy is to be utilized. The foundation system of a building is not relevant to a building's orientation on the site.

31. **A** The absence of a storm drainage system would cause all surface water to drain haphazardly instead of being properly conducted off site. A flat site would also drain poorly, allowing the water to pond rather than flow. The existence of a high water table actually indicates poor drainage since relatively little water seeps into the ground before it reaches the saturation point. Both the presence of dense groundcover and a flowing stream would indicate good drainage. Groundcover would slow the water flow and allow absorption into the earth and the stream would act as an efficient surface drainage system.

32. **C** The conclusion of the programming phase results in the final program, which is used as the basis for schematic design. The program expresses the space requirements, determined by the client's needs and objectives, as net usable floor area for various activities. The other means, dimensions, proportions, and configurations, are expressions of the program that render the shapes and relationships of spaces that are the result of the schematic design phase (which comes later).

33. **C** The cost per use unit is a standard basis for preliminary cost estimating in the pre-design phase. The cost of a school would be figured on a per student basis, the cost of a prison on a per inmate basis, and the cost of a medical facility on a per bed basis. The exception is pedestrians, who are rarely considered a use class for any type of facility. Cost estimating on a use unit basis is quick and effective but can be unreliable if the planned building is unconventional.

34. **D** The city has the right to acquire the property under eminent domain and the owner has the right to sell the property at an equitable price. If they cannot agree on a price, it will be decided by a court, not the redevelopment agency. That price will represent the fair market value of the land and any improvements thereon, not withstanding its vacancy. The city, nonetheless, has the right to take the property legally and have the equitable price determined later.

35. **A** Local governmental agencies such as cities and counties enact zoning ordinances to regulate and control land use for the public health, safety, and welfare. Except for minimizing fire danger, any of the results listed may be achieved by zoning ordinances. Minimizing fire danger is normally achieved by building codes, not planning codes.

36. **B** The complexity of a project, rather than its size, cost, or quality, is the prime factor for the architect to consider when staffing and scheduling the project's completion in his or her office. A large and/or costly project may still be simple and conventional in nature, requiring less production time than one that is more complex. The quality of a project is achieved through the architect's skill and the available building budget, not the amount of staff time spent in producing the design.

37. **B** The main objective of a building program itself is to define the essential building problem. The programming process actually discovers the building's function and purpose in order to better define the problem. The schematic design phase uses the completed program to determine the building solution and decide on the actual building form.

38. **C** Building industry standards have generally established the use of the 36-inch doorway. Smaller doorway widths have accommodated traditional use and typical human dimensions, and code requirements generally refer only to exit requirements for doors.

39. **A** Regular forms, compact arrangements, and high densities reduce the construction cost of a building design due to simplicity, efficiency, and conservation. Harmonious proportions, while possibly desirable, do not lower the construction cost and may, in fact, lead to extraneous costs.

40. **D** One of the most effective methods to save construction time is to reduce the critical path time, thereby reducing the whole schedule. Because inefficiency is increased due to the need for additional supervision and coordination of overtime work, reducing the time for critical activities will likely increase direct costs. Maintaining quality control with shortened schedules is more difficult, so quality will generally be affected in some way. The float time is the difference between the critical path and any other path, so as the critical path is reduced, the float time will also be reduced.

41. **A** Building codes use the terms *exit* and *means of egress* interchangeably. A building may have more legal ways out than the number required by code. There may be many ways out of a building in case of emergency that are not up to the code-required standards for exits and means of egress.

42. **C** Proposed buildings are classified by type of construction, degree of fire hazard and fire resistance, and occupancy type. Land use is not addressed in building codes, but rather in planning and zoning regulations.

43. **C** If today's cost index is 1050 and is projected to be 1260 when the building is to be built, dividing 1260 by 1050 gives a projected 20 percent increase in costs. Increasing today's cost of $90.00 per square foot by 20 percent yields $108.00 per square foot.

44. **B** The catchment area is also known as the *market area* or *trade area*. It is the tributary area from which a facility derives its user population. The catchment area can vary in size depending on the convenience and travel time to reach the center. It determines the actual viable type and size requirement of the center itself to serve the user population.

45. **C** FAR stands for floor area ratio, the allowable building area expressed as a multiple of the site area. Since the site is 100,000 square feet, multiplying by a FAR of 4.0 yields a maximum building area of 400,000 square feet. In this case, however, although the site is 100,000 square feet, only half (50,000 square feet) can be used for the building. Therefore, dividing the allowable 400,000 square feet by 50,000 square feet results in the design needing eight stories.

46. **B** The prime objectives of well-designed pedestrian circulation are safety, security, convenience, and comfort. Speed is not as relevant to pedestrian as it is to vehicular circulation. Economy is not a primary goal, nor is permanence, though both are obviously desirable considerations.

47. **A** According to ANSI standards, a handicapped-accessible route is a continuous, unobstructed path connecting all accessible areas of a building for people with any type of physical, sensory, or mental disability (items II, IV, and V). Accessible paths must be designed for both interior and exterior locations, so item III is incorrect. Objects may protrude to various extents depending on the height of the projection.

48. **B** To arrive at the solution, the required parking first needs to be calculated. If the building has 80,000 square feet with a 0.8 efficiency ratio, its occupied area is

$$(80,000\,\text{ft}^2)(0.8) = 64,000\,\text{ft}^2$$

$$\frac{64,000\,\text{ft}^2}{\dfrac{300\,\text{ft}^2}{\text{car}}} = 213 \text{ car spaces required}$$

The standard area allowance per car for parking areas (including aisles) is 400 square feet per car.

$$\left(400\,\frac{\text{ft}^2}{\text{car}}\right)(213\,\text{cars}) = 85,200\,\text{ft}^2$$

Since an acre of land contains 43,560 square feet,

$$\frac{85,200\,\text{ft}^2}{43,560\,\dfrac{\text{ft}^2}{\text{acre}}} = 1.96\,\text{acres}$$

The closest answer is 2.0 acres.

49. **C** Heat transmission through a material or assembly of materials is measured by the U-factor, which is the inverse of the R-value. The higher the U-factor, the faster the rate of heat loss or heat gain. Higher numbers reflect a material's tendency to have rapid heat loss or gain. Therefore, materials with high U-factors should only be used in areas that have moderate climates all year long.

50. **C** In the initial programming stage, the actual areas and volumes of the project along with other development costs are yet to be defined. This factor renders most methods of accurate cost estimating insufficient. For programming purposes, the most reliable method for projecting costs at this preliminary stage is to research historical data on similar projects for comparison to the one being designed.

General Structures Division

Sample Examination

1. For which of the following reasons are long spans used?

      I. improved resistance to lateral loads
      II. functional flexibility
      III. aesthetic effect
      IV. unobstructed visibility
      V. economy

  A. I, II, and III
  B. II, III, and IV
  C. III, IV, and V
  D. II, III, and V

2. In observing the preparation for the pouring of concrete for a column footing, the architect notices that the bottom of the excavation is frozen due to the cold weather. What should the contractor do?

  A. Add additional reinforcing steel to the footing and pour.
  B. Excavate the frozen ground and pour.
  C. Use a portable heating apparatus to thaw the frozen ground and pour.
  D. Wait for warmer weather to thaw the frozen ground and then pour.

3. For a material such as steel, what is the ratio of unit stress to unit strain called?

  A. the modulus of elasticity
  B. the modulus of resilience
  C. the modulus of rigidity
  D. Poisson's ratio

4. What is the disadvantage of a simple beam structure compared with a continuous beam structure?

  A. It requires more complex calculations.
  B. It requires more complex connections.
  C. It has more deflection.
  D. It has more shear.

5. A glulam beam that is 12 inches deep is rated at 2200 pounds per square inch for its allowable unit bending stress. What is the allowable unit bending stress for a glulam beam 18 inches deep of the same grade?

  A. less than 2200 psi
  B. 2200 psi
  C. more than 2200 psi
  D. not enough information to calculate

6. For structural purposes, which species and grade of wood is best to use for floor joists?

  A. redwood, no. 1
  B. Douglas fir, no. 1
  C. spruce, no. 1
  D. cedar, no. 1

7. A wood column is axially loaded. The calculation for its deformation requires four factors. Cross-sectional area, the applied load, and the member's length are three. What is the fourth?

  A. weight
  B. moment of inertia
  C. radius of gyration
  D. modulus of elasticity

8. The compressive strength of concrete for a foundation is specified to be 3000 pounds per square inch. A test cylinder taken 7 days ago has a strength of 2000 pounds per square inch. What should the architect do in this situation?

    A. Wait for an additional 21 days.
    B. Order additional testing of samples.
    C. Stop work and advise the contractor to remove the concrete.
    D. Revise the concrete mix design.

9. What is the maximum slump of concrete used in a driveway?

    A. 2 inches
    B. 3 inches
    C. 4 inches
    D. 6 inches

10. In the design of a wood beam that is 15 inches deep and 30 feet long, the deflection is calculated to be $3/4$ inch. What should be changed in the design to limit deflection to $1/2$ inch?

    A. Use a beam with a 50 percent larger section modulus.
    B. Shorten the span to 20 feet.
    C. Use a beam with a moment of inertia 50 percent greater.
    D. Use a beam with a 150 percent larger modulus of elasticity.

11. In the following cantilevered beam, what is the left reaction?

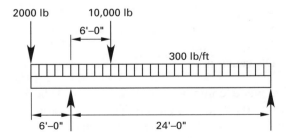

    A. 4200 pounds
    B. 15,625 pounds
    C. 16,800 pounds
    D. 20,625 pounds

12. A circular concrete footing pad supporting a steel column is overstressed in shear. What should be done to properly support the column loads?

    A. Increase the pad thickness.
    B. Increase the pad diameter and area.
    C. Increase the amount of reinforcing steel.
    D. Increase the size of the steel column.

13. As designed, a reinforced concrete beam has too much deflection. The load cannot be reduced or redistributed. What would be the most efficient design method to reduce the beam's deflection?

    A. Widen the beam.
    B. Deepen the beam.
    C. Add more steel reinforcement.
    D. Increase the strength of the concrete.

14. A $3/4$-inch diameter steel reinforcing bar is 20 feet long. Under load, it elongates 0.10 inch. The modulus of elasticity of the steel equals 40 million pounds per square inch. What is the unit stress in the bar?

    A. 12,083 psi
    B. 15,000 psi
    C. 16,667 psi
    D. 20,000 psi

15. Which of the following is most important to provide the most economical and least expensive framing system of reinforced concrete?

    A. Formwork and reinforcement are simple, uniform, and repetitive.
    B. Concrete areas in tension are replaced with voids to reduce the weight of the system.
    C. Vertical loads are taken by bearing walls; lateral loads are taken by rigid frames.
    D. Large reinforcing bars are used to keep their number to a minimum.

16. In the following simple beam, what is the maximum moment?

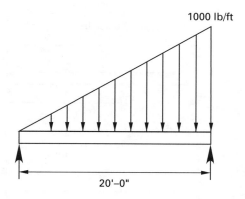

1000 lb/ft

20'-0"

    A. 19,233 ft-lb
    B. 20,000 ft-lb
    C. 25,664 ft-lb
    D. 51,288 ft-lb

17. What is the primary purpose of a base plate under a structural steel column?

    A. to provide a means to attach the column to the footing
    B. to distribute the column load over a sufficient area of the footing
    C. to provide a template for the column anchor bolts
    D. to isolate the steel from the concrete

18. The architect is observing the placement of the reinforcement in formwork for footings. Which of the following is unacceptable and must be removed from the steel bars before concrete is placed?

    A. dirt
    B. dirt or oil
    C. dirt, oil, or rust
    D. dirt, oil, rust, or scale

19. As wood members dry and lose moisture, they shrink. Which of the following is true regarding shrinkage?

    A. Joists shrink most in their depth.
    B. Studs shrink most in their length.
    C. Logs shrink most radially.
    D. Gluelams shrink more than solid wood beams.

20. Why is the bottom of a caisson belled?

    A. to provide working space for placing reinforcement at the bottom
    B. to provide for drainage at the bottom
    C. to provide additional bearing area to carry the loads
    D. to provide additional lateral resistance for the caisson

21. If a structure is in static equilibrium, which of the following statements is incorrect?

    A. The resultant force passes through the center.
    B. The sum of the moments equals zero.
    C. The sum of the forces in any direction equals zero.
    D. The resultant force equals zero.

22. The dome of what building was the longest-spanning concrete structure until the twentieth century?

    A. the Parthenon
    B. the Pantheon
    C. the Baths of Caracalla
    D. St. Peter's Basilica

23. A 4-inch concrete slab, 10 feet long, is restrained from any movement. If the slab temperature increases $30°F$, what amount and type of internal stress is created in the slab? (Assume that the modulus of elasticity is 2,900,000 pounds per square inch and the coefficient of expansion is 0.0000050/°F.)

    A. 435 psi tension
    B. 435 psi compression
    C. 4350 psi tension
    D. 4350 psi compression

24. To what does the term *pile cap* refer?

    A. the structural bearing load capacity of a pile
    B. a reinforced concrete beam spanning between piles and distributing the loads upon it to the piles
    C. a device on the top of a pile to protect it from damage during the actual process of driving the pile into the earth
    D. a reinforced concrete slab spanning piles and distributing the loads upon it to the piles

25. Which statement concerning braced frames is correct?

    A. Either steel or concrete can be used.
    B. Braced frames are less rigid than rigid frames.
    C. Braced frame connectors resist bending moments.
    D. Braced frames resist only lateral loads.

26. What term is used to describe the ratio between the effective length of a column and its least radius of gyration?

    A. Poisson's ratio
    B. Young's modulus
    C. slenderness ratio
    D. section modulus

27. What are stirrups used for in a concrete beam?

    A. compressive reinforcement
    B. proper spacing of the reinforcing during the pour
    C. resistance to bending due to moment created by the loads
    D. resistance to shear when concrete is overstressed

28. Which of the following buildings employ bundled structural tubular framing systems?

    I. World Trade Center, New York City
    II. Pompidou Center, Paris
    III. Sears Tower, Chicago
    IV. John Hancock Building, Boston
    V. Transamerica Pyramid, San Francisco

    A. I and III
    B. I, II, III, and IV
    C. I, III, and IV
    D. I, II, III, IV, and V

29. A steel column is supported by a concrete pad footing. The load on the column is 125 kips. F_c for concrete is 4000 pounds per square inch. The allowable soil bearing pressure is 2.5 tons per square foot. If the weight of the column and pad are not considered, what size pad should be designed?

    A. $3'\text{-}6''$ square
    B. $5'\text{-}0''$ square
    C. $5'\text{-}6''$ square
    D. $7'\text{-}2''$ square

30. Which of the following beam loading diagrams produces the most deflection?

A.
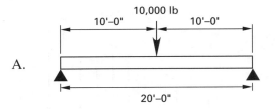

B.
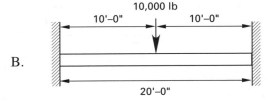

C.
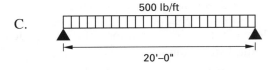

D.
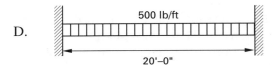

31. What is a space frame?

    A. a moment-resisting frame
    B. a two-way system of trusses
    C. a two-way system of rigid frames
    D. a three-dimensional structural system

32. Long-span construction would most likely be designed for which types of buildings?

    I. auditoriums
    II. gymnasiums
    III. libraries
    IV. speculative office buildings
    V. airport terminals

    A. I and II
    B. I, II, and IV
    C. II, III, and IV
    D. II, IV, and V

33. In the following diagram, what is the resulting moment of the three forces about point A?

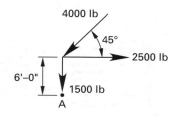

A. 1968 ft-lb
B. 9000 ft-lb
C. 15,000 ft-lb
D. 31,973 ft-lb

34. Who designed the first skyscraper?

A. Robert Maillart
B. Elisha Graves Otis
C. William LeBaron Jenney
D. Louis Sullivan

35. The design of an office building has a structural bay spacing of 20 feet. The owner wants to double the bay spacing to provide more flexibility for tenants. By approximately what percentage will the total construction cost of the building increase?

A. 2 percent
B. 6 percent
C. 10 percent
D. 25 percent

36. Steel joists, 6 feet on center, are used to support the roof of a building. The joists, in turn, are supported by joist girders, 40 feet long, spaced 50 feet apart. Total live and dead loads, including the weight of the steel structure, are 50 pounds per square foot. What is the load at each point of connection between the joist and the girder?

A. 6.0 kips
B. 7.5 kips
C. 12.0 kips
D. 15.0 kips

37. On a site visit, the architect is asked by the contractor to approve the plywood sheathing used for an interior subfloor. The trademark on the plywood reads:

APA Rated Sheathing
Structural 1
24/0—1/2 Inch
Exposure 1

What action should the architect take?

A. Accept the plywood if the floor joist spacing is not more than 16 inches on center.
B. Accept the plywood if the floor joist spacing is not more than 24 inches on center.
C. Require a testing agency to determine if the plywood is acceptable.
D. Reject the plywood.

38. What type of structure is best for supporting concentrated loads?

A. domes
B. arches
C. beams
D. trusses

39. The domed roof of a sports stadium is constructed with a ring at the center and a ring at the perimeter. The two rings are connected by a series of arched ribs, radial in plan. Which is the correct statement?

A. The center ring is in compression.
B. The perimeter ring is in compression.
C. Both rings are in compression.
D. Neither ring is in compression.

40. Which statement concerning membrane roof structures is incorrect?

A. The occupied space under a membrane roof structure need not be pressurized.
B. A membrane roof changes shape to adapt to changing loads.
C. A pillow roof is a type of membrane structure.
D. A membrane roof cannot resist tension forces.

41. Which of the following is true for long-span cable roof structures?

    A. High-strength steel cable is about 10 times as strong as structural steel.

    B. As the span increases, the cost per unit of roof area decreases.

    C. Cables are subject to buckling and must be restrained.

    D. Cables assume hyperbolic shapes when uniform loads are applied.

42. The following beam is a Douglas fir, Select Structural grade, with loads and supports as shown. The maximum shear is 3000 pounds, and the maximum moment is 15,000 ft-lb. The allowable bending stress is 1200 pounds per square inch, and the allowable shear stress is 90 pounds per square inch. To properly size a beam that will support the loads, what is the required area and section modulus?

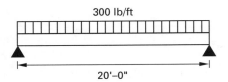

    A. $A = 33.3 \text{ in}^2$, $S = 12.5 \text{ in}^3$
    B. $A = 33.3 \text{ in}^2$, $S = 150.0 \text{ in}^3$
    C. $A = 50.0 \text{ in}^2$, $S = 150.0 \text{ in}^3$
    D. $A = 50.0 \text{ in}^2$, $S = 12.5 \text{ in}^3$

43. Which of the following statements regarding prestressed concrete is correct?

    A. Prestressing causes stresses opposite to those caused by live and dead loads.

    B. Pretensioned members require secure end anchorages.

    C. Prestressing eliminates creep and shrinkage in the concrete.

    D. Posttensioning is not a method of prestressing concrete.

44. Which of the following diagrams represents the flexural stress distribution of a rectangular solid sawn wood beam?

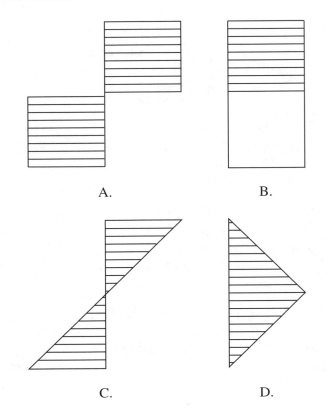

45. Which of the following statements regarding a retaining wall where the resisting moment from the dead load of the wall equals the overturning moment from earth pressure behind the wall is correct?

    A. Additional steel reinforcement should be used.
    B. A keyed footing should be used.
    C. A wider footing should be used.
    D. The design is adequate.

46. A beam is loaded as shown. If the beam's weight is negligible, what is the reaction at R_2?

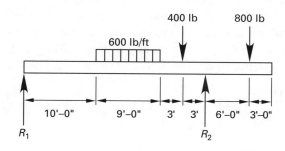

A. 3300 pounds
B. 4476 pounds
C. 5448 pounds
D. 5594 pounds

47. What is the resultant force of the two forces shown?

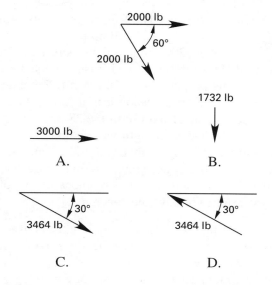

48. Which is the correct statement concerning live load?

   A. Live load does not include wind loads and seismic loads.
   B. Live load may not be less than dead load.
   C. Long-span structures must be designed for higher live loads than conventional structures.
   D. Live load can be neglected if it is less than dead load and is approved by the building official.

49. Which of the following is not used in determining the load-bearing capacity of a rectangular wood column?

   A. the dimensions of the column section
   B. the radius of gyration of the column section
   C. the unbraced height of the column
   D. the species of wood used in the column

50. For composite design, which of the following statements is correct?

   A. Composite design is generally more expensive than conventional steel framing.
   B. Composite design uses shear connectors that can fully utilize the ultimate capacity of the steel or concrete, whichever is greater.
   C. Composite design should only be used when conventional steel framing cannot support the design loads.
   D. Deflection is more critical in composite design than in conventional steel framing.

Examination Answers with Explanations

1. B Long spans provide functional flexibility since the enclosed space is easily modified without disrupting interior structural systems. The aesthetic appeal of vast, column-free spaces is an important consideration and advantage. In public spaces, especially those used for entertainment and cultural affairs, the lack of columns and bearing walls in long-span structures provides unobstructed visibility. It is not true, though, that long spans provide better resistance to lateral loads, nor are they economical when compared with short spans.

2. B Concrete should never be placed on frozen ground because the ground will shrink when it thaws and cause the concrete to crack and weaken. Adding additional reinforcing will not prevent the ground from shrinking. Thawing the ground by heating it, though possible, is not a good choice. If the ground is frozen at the time of the pour, it is likely to freeze again in the future. The bottoms of footings should always be placed below the frost line to prevent damage. Waiting for warmer weather is not practical since that would cause an inordinate delay in the construction. The proper procedure would be to excavate below the frozen ground to place the bottom of the footing below the frost line, eliminating the present and future problem.

3. A The ratio of unit stress to unit strain in any material is called its *modulus of elasticity*. Unit stress is the stress per unit area measured in pounds per square inch. Unit strain is the total shortening or lengthening of a member divided by its length. The higher the E value, the greater its stiffness or resistance to deformation.

4. C Simple beams have more deflection than continuous beams, which is a disadvantage to using simple beams. Continuous beams require more complex calculations and more complex connections than simple beams. Simple beams generally have more maximum moment, but continuous beams usually have more maximum shear.

5. A The full allowable unit bending stress is used in glulams up to 12 inches deep. Beams more than 12 inches deep must reduce the allowable unit bending stress by a size factor related to their depth. Therefore, the allowable unit stress would be less than 2200 pounds per square inch.

6. B Redwood is usually used when the structure will be exposed to the weather and durability is the main consideration. Douglas fir is the strongest species and is commonly used in construction. Spruce is lightweight with low strength, so it is not normally used for structural building applications. Cedar, like redwood, is durable when exposed to the weather, lightweight and low in strength, and is mainly used for siding and trim (as is redwood).

7. D

$$\text{deformation} = \frac{PL}{AE}$$

P is the concentrated load, L is the length, A is the cross-sectional area, and E represents the modulus of elasticity. The modulus of elasticity is the measure of how stiff the material is (in this case, wood) and determines its resistance to deformation under load.

8. A Compressive strength is specified to be reached at the end of 28 days. At the end of 7 days, concrete usually reaches approximately 60–70 percent of its ultimate compressive strength. Since 3000 pounds per square inch was specified, 2000 pounds per square inch is about 67 percent of the ultimate, so it is assumed that the concrete is curing properly and will reach full strength as required. The correct response is to do nothing and wait an additional 21 days until the 28-day strength is known. If the 7-day strength was significantly lower, then additional testing might be advisable, and the concrete mix design may need revision. In no case does the architect have the authority to stop the work and direct the contractor to remove the concrete.

9. C A slump test is used to measure the consistency of concrete. Less slump means the mix is stiffer; more slump means the mix is wetter. Generally, 4 inches is the maximum acceptable slump for concrete used in construction.

10. C

$$\text{deflection} = \frac{KwL^3}{EI}$$

K represents the load factor, w the total uniform load, L the length, E the modulus of elasticity, and I the moment of inertia. No formal calculation is necessary. Only the relationships in the formula need to be known. Since both E and I are in the denominator of the equation, either one should be increased by 50 percent to decrease the deflection by 33 percent (0.75 inch/0.50 inch = 1.50). The correct answer is to increase the moment of inertia by 50 percent.

11. B In structural beam design, the sum of the moments must be zero at any reaction point. To find the left reaction, the moments about the right reaction must be calculated. Therefore,

$$\sum M = 0$$

$$\left(-300 \, \frac{\text{lb}}{\text{ft}}\right)(24 \, \text{ft} + 6 \, \text{ft})\left(\frac{30 \, \text{ft}}{2}\right)$$
$$- (10,000 \, \text{lb})(24 \, \text{ft} - 6 \, \text{ft})$$
$$- (2000 \, \text{lb})(24 \, \text{ft} + 6 \, \text{ft}) + R_L(24 \, \text{ft}) = 0$$

Therefore, to solve for R_L,

$$R_L = \frac{\left(300 \, \frac{\text{lb}}{\text{ft}}\right)(30 \, \text{ft})(15 \, \text{ft}) + (10,000 \, \text{lb})(18 \, \text{ft}) + (2000 \, \text{lb})(30 \, \text{ft})}{24 \, \text{ft}}$$

$$= \frac{135,000 \, \text{ft-lb} + 180,000 \, \text{ft-lb} + 60,000 \, \text{ft-lb}}{24 \, \text{ft}}$$

$$= \frac{375,000 \, \text{ft-lb}}{24 \, \text{ft}}$$

$$= 15,625 \, \text{lb}$$

12. A The column loads, the column size, and the pad thickness all determine the amount of shear stress in the footing itself. The amount and size of steel reinforcement does not enter into the calculation for shear stress. Increasing the pad area causes only a marginal decrease in the shear stress. The only way to properly reduce the shear stress would be to increase the pad thickness. The increased thickness would then provide more concrete to resist the shear stress itself.

13. B Each of the design methods listed will reduce the deflection of a reinforced concrete beam. Making the beam wider or deeper will increase the moment of inertia. Additional reinforcing steel will decrease the deflection, as will higher-strength concrete. The most efficient way, however, is to increase the beam depth. Since the moment of inertia is proportional to depth^3, a small, cost-effective increase in depth yields a great increase in strength, thus reducing the deflection. For example, if the depth is increased by 10 percent, 1.1^3 results in 1.33, giving a 33 percent decrease in deflection.

14. C Load divided by area (P/A) represents unit stress. Deformation divided by length in inches (D/L) represents unit strain. The ratio of unit stress to unit strain is equal to the modulus of elasticity, up to the elastic limit. Therefore,

$$\frac{\frac{P}{A}}{\frac{D}{L}} = E \quad \text{or} \quad D = \frac{PL}{AE} \quad \text{or} \quad \frac{P}{A} = \frac{DE}{L}$$

To solve the equation for unit stress,

$$\frac{P}{A} = \frac{(0.10 \, \text{in})\left(40,000,000 \, \frac{\text{lb}}{\text{in}^2}\right)}{(20 \, \text{ft})\left(12 \, \frac{\text{in}}{\text{ft}}\right)}$$

$$= 16,667 \, \frac{\text{lb}}{\text{in}^2} \, (\text{psi})$$

Note that deflection and length are in inches, and stress and modulus of elasticity are in pounds per square inch. All units must be consistent with one another.

15. A Formwork and reinforcing are a large part of the labor and material costs of any concrete framing system. Keeping the formwork simple and uniform and using reusable forms in a repetitive manner allows the labor and material costs of forming the system to remain economical. The same is true for steel reinforcing, thus the correct answer is choice A. Replacing areas in tension with voids is characteristic of a waffle slab system, which is not the most economical due to the formwork involved. In low rises, vertical and horizontal forces are taken by bearing walls; whereas high rises often employ rigid frames to carry both loadings. The amount of reinforcing is important, but it can increase the amount of concrete needed. The additional concrete adds to the dead weight of the system and increases foundation sizes, which increases material and labor costs.

16. C To solve for the maximum moment, the left reaction must first be determined by taking moments around the right reaction, (the sum of the moments is always zero). Therefore,

$$\left(-1000 \, \frac{\text{lb}}{\text{ft}}\right)\left(\frac{20 \, \text{ft}}{2}\right)\left(\frac{20 \, \text{ft}}{3}\right) + R_L(20 \, \text{ft}) = 0$$

$$R_L = \frac{\left(1000 \, \frac{\text{lb}}{\text{ft}}\right)(10 \, \text{ft})(6.666 \, \text{ft})}{20 \, \text{ft}} = 3333 \, \text{lb}$$

The maximum moment occurs where the shear becomes zero. The load is increasing at the rate of

$$\frac{1000 \, \text{lb}}{20 \, \text{ft}} = 50 \, \text{lb/ft}$$

Next, find the distance x from the left reaction to the point of zero shear.

$$\left(50 \, \frac{\text{lb}}{\text{ft}}\right)(x \, \text{ft})\left(\frac{x \, \text{ft}}{2}\right) = 3333 \, \text{ft-lb}$$

Solving for x,

$$x^2 = \frac{3333 \, \text{ft-lb}}{25 \, \dfrac{\text{lb}}{\text{ft}}} = 133.32 \, \text{ft}^2$$

$$x = \sqrt{133.32 \, \text{ft}^2} = 11.55 \, \text{ft}$$

The maximum moment equals

$$(3333 \, \text{lb})(11.55 \, \text{ft})$$

$$- (3333 \, \text{lb})\left(\frac{11.55 \, \text{ft}}{3}\right) = 25{,}664 \, \text{ft-lb}$$

17. B The loads taken by a steel column are relatively high compared to the bearing capacity of the concrete footing. Therefore, a base plate is used to distribute the column loads evenly over a larger area to avoid overstressing the concrete. The area of the base plate is calculated using the column loads and the allowable compressive strength of the concrete supporting them.

18. B Dirt, oil, or other nonmetallic coatings must be removed before concrete is placed so that the bond between the steel and the concrete is not adversely affected. Rust and scale, often removed during the handling and placement of the steel, actually improve the bond and so are considered satisfactory.

19. A Wood shrinks most in the direction of the annual growth rings (tangentially), less across the rings (radially), and least along the grain (longitudinally). Therefore, studs and logs shrink very little compared with the shrinking of joists across their depth. Glue-lams are made with seasoned lumber and are designed for very little shrinkage, which is one reason they are used in place of solid lumber.

20. C The purpose of belling the caisson bottom is to provide additional bearing area to support the imposed loads on the caisson itself. Sometimes the bearing values of soils near the surface are low because of poor soil, but at lower depths, denser soils are found capable of higher bearing values. To take maximum advantage of these higher bearing pressures with economically designed caissons, a smaller shaft is drilled through the poor soils until the denser layer is reached. A special attachment on the drill allows the shaft to be enlarged

at the bottom in the shape of a bell. This larger belled area provides greater bearing area to support the applied caisson loads.

21. A If a structure is in static equilibrium, there are no unbalanced forces acting on it. There are no unbalanced moments acting on it either. Choice A is incorrect because if there is a resultant force on a structure, acting anywhere, it will move, causing the structure to be nonstatic and out of equilibrium.

22. B The Pantheon was one of the greatest achievements of Roman architecture and engineering. Although the Romans regularly used concrete in their structures, it was unreinforced because they had no steel. To take advantage of the properties of concrete, the structures had to be designed to be in compression. Thus, arches and domes were frequently used. The dome of the Pantheon spanned 142 feet with unreinforced concrete; it was the longest spanning dome until 1913. When reinforced concrete came into use, even longer spans became possible.

23. B If the slab is restrained from any movement, it will try to expand due to the temperature increase and its supports will try to compress it back to its original length, creating internal stress.

$$\begin{array}{l} \text{expansion due} \\ \text{to temperature} \end{array} = \alpha L \Delta t = \begin{array}{l} \text{compression due} \\ \text{to the loads} \end{array}$$

$$= \frac{PL}{AE}$$

Solving for the stress,

$$\frac{P}{A} = \alpha E \Delta t$$

α is the coefficient of expansion ($0.0000050/°\text{F}$), E is the modulus of elasticity ($2{,}900{,}000$ psi), and Δt is the temperature differential, $30°\text{F}$.

$$\frac{P}{A} = \left(\frac{0.0000050}{°\text{F}}\right)(2{,}900{,}000 \, \text{psi})(30°\text{F})$$

$$= 435 \, \text{psi} \quad [\text{in compression}]$$

24. D Usually single piles do not have adequate bearing capacity by themselves. In that case, groups of piles are used to support vertical loads. The loads are distributed by means of a pile cap spanning several piles. Choice B refers to a grade beam and choices A and C are incorrect.

25. **C**   Braced frames (or K-frames) are constructed with steel members forming diagonal braces to act in both tension and compression between beams and columns. Concrete is not used for braced frames because it is so weak in tension. Braced frames usually have bolted connections, which are not rigid like welded connections. Braced frames are designed to create a triangulated system of connections to resist lateral shear and bending moments. Since they efficiently resist both vertical and lateral (seismic) loadings, they are employed in both low-rise and high-rise construction.

26. **C**   In the design of columns, the ratio of the effective length, l, to its least radius of gyration, r, is known as the slenderness ratio.

27. **D**   Small diameter bars in a U-shape placed transversely in a beam or column are known as stirrups. Their purpose is to reinforce the concrete in areas where shear stresses exceed the capability of concrete. They are not used for compressive reinforcement or resistance to bending, both of which are taken by the longitudinal bars. Stirrups have a structural design purpose, whereas ties are used to maintain proper spacing between reinforcing bars during the pouring of concrete.

28. **A**   Only a few high-rise buildings use structural tubular framing systems. Perimeter walls form a huge hollow tube cantilevering out of the ground to resist wind and seismic forces. The World Trade Center and the Sears Tower are the only buildings listed which are tubular buildings. The others are examples of moment-resisting space frames and rigid frame structures.

29. **B**   The column load is divided by the soil bearing pressure to find the area of the footing.

$$125 \text{ kips} = 125,000 \text{ lb}$$

Convert 2.5 tons per square foot to a consistent unit of measure.

$$\left(2.5 \, \frac{\text{tons}}{\text{ft}^2}\right)\left(2000 \, \frac{\text{lb}}{\text{ton}}\right) = 5000 \, \frac{\text{lb}}{\text{ft}^2} \quad (\text{psf}) \quad \left[\begin{array}{c} \text{soil bearing} \\ \text{capacity} \end{array}\right]$$

$$\frac{125,000 \text{ lb}}{5000 \, \frac{\text{lb}}{\text{ft}^2}} = 25 \text{ ft}^2 \quad [\text{the area of the footing}]$$

Since the square root of 25 is 5, the pad needs to be 5'-0" square.

30. **A**   This question asks only which beam/load condition produces the most deflection. It is not necessary to calculate the actual deflection. Conceptually, simply-supported beams (choices A and C) deflect more than fixed-end beams (choices B and D). Likewise, concentrated loads (choices A and B) cause more deflection than uniformly distributed loads (choices C and D). Therefore, the most deflection will occur in a simply-supported beam with a concentrated load.

31. **B**   A space frame is a series of two-way trusses, equally deep, that intersect in a grid pattern and are connected at their points of intersection. Both directions of trusses are used to support loads and the connections transfer loads so that the system works together as a unit. Moment-resisting frames are not necessarily space frames, as they do not have to be intersecting trusses. The same is true of two-way rigid frames. All structural systems are three-dimensional, so choice D is incorrect as well.

32. **A**   Long-span construction is used where column-free space is required, such as in auditoriums, gymnasiums, and other areas of public assembly where maximum flexibility and visibility is desired. Libraries, speculative office buildings, and airport terminals do not require the same flexibility and visibility of column-free space, so long-span structures are not necessary.

33. **A**   The total resulting moment about point A is the algebraic sum of the moments caused by all the forces. Each moment about a point is calculated by multiplying the force by the distance from the point. The 1500-lb vertical force is acting through point A, so its moment is zero and it is disregarded. The 2500-lb horizontal force is acting 6'-0" away from point A and produces 15,000 ft-lb of moment in a clockwise direction [(2500 lb)(6 ft) = 15,000 ft-lb]. The 4000-lb force on a 45° diagonal needs to first be resolved into its vertical and horizontal components. The vertical component is

$$(4000 \text{ lb})(\sin 45°) = 2828 \text{ lb}$$

Since the force is acting through point A, it creates no moment and is disregarded. The horizontal component is

$$(4000 \text{ lb})(\cos 45°) = 2828 \text{ lb}$$

This component acts in a counterclockwise direction, producing 16,968 ft-lb of moment [(2828 lb)(6 ft) = 16,968 ft-lb]. Summing the moments about point A in each direction yields the correct answer.

$$16,968 \text{ ft-lb} - 15,000 \text{ ft-lb} = 1968 \text{ ft-lb}$$

34. **C**   William LeBaron Jenney designed the Home Insurance Co. Building, the first skyscraper, in 1883. Robert Maillart was a Swiss engineer who designed

arched concrete bridges. Skyscrapers were made possible by the invention of the elevator by Elisha Graves Otis. Louis Sullivan, a noted Chicago architect, is famous for his cast-iron framed buildings which were among the first skyscrapers, but the Home Insurance Co. was built first.

35. **B** Typically, structural systems in a building represent approximately 25 percent of the total construction cost. If the spans of the structural bays are doubled, the costs for the structural system would probably increase by about 20–30 percent. Since structural costs represent 25 percent of total costs, the increase will range from 5 percent [(0.20)(0.25)] to 7.5 percent [(0.30)(0.25)]. Six percent is the average, therefore choice B is correct.

36. **B** Each steel joist distributes half its total load to each endpoint where it is connected to each girder. The total load on each joist equals the load (in pounds per square foot), times the length (the distance between girders) times the spacing (for the tributary area). Therefore, each joist carries

$$\left(50 \; \frac{\text{lb}}{\text{ft}^2}\right)(50 \text{ ft})(6 \text{ ft}) = 15{,}000 \text{ lb (or 15 kips)}$$

Half of this load is carried by the girder at each end, therefore the correct answer is 7.5 kips. The length of the girder itself is immaterial to the question.

37. **D** All structural plywood is required to be graded and marked as to its usage. Usually the trademark is of the American Plywood Association (APA). The span rating is usually given in two numbers, the first for use as roof sheathing, the second for floor sheathing (e.g., 48/24). The trademark on the plywood in the question specifies the span rating to be 24/0, meaning that it can span 24 inches for roofs but is not permitted to be used for floor sheathing. (If permitted for floor sheathing, the span rating would be noted.) The proper procedure would be for the architect to reject the sheathing as unacceptable for use as floor sheathing.

38. **D** Generally, concentrated loads cause large bending moments in a structure. Domes, arches, and beams are all better suited to support uniformly distributed loads. Trusses are usually used to support large concentrated loads because they are best at resisting bending moments. The bending moment from concentrated loads causes compressive stress in the top chord of a truss, tensile stress in the bottom chord, and either tension or compression in the web members.

39. **A** The radial ribs are arched, so they behave as arches in resisting the roof loads. They exhibit an outward thrust at their supports, causing tension in the perimeter ring as it tries to open up. At the same time, this thrust tends to compress the center ring.

40. **D** Although many membranes are air-supported structures, it is not necessary to pressurize the occupied space below them. Instead, architects use double membranes, which are only pressurized within the roof structure itself. A membrane roof does change shape as the loads (such as wind loads) change. A pillow roof is another term for a double-membrane roof, pressurized within for support. A membrane cannot resist compression, shear, or moment. The only force a membrane roof can resist is tension.

41. **B** High-strength cable has twice the strength of structural steel, not 10 times. Cables are in constant tension and, therefore, are not subject to buckling, so they need not be restrained. When they are uniformly loaded, cables assume parabolic shapes, not hyperbolic. The connections, anchorage, and fittings represent the major expense of a cable roof, not the cables themselves. These elements remain essentially constant even when the spans increase. Since the cables are a relatively small part of the cost, the unit cost per square foot of roof area decreases as the span increases.

42. **C** The formula to find the area required to resist shear stress is

$$A = \frac{3V}{2f_v}$$
$$V = 3000 \text{ lb}$$
$$f_v = 90 \text{ psi}$$

Therefore,

$$A = \frac{(3)(3000 \text{ lb})}{(2)\left(90 \; \dfrac{\text{lb}}{\text{in}^2}\right)} = \frac{9000 \text{ lb}}{180 \; \dfrac{\text{lb}}{\text{in}^2}}$$
$$= 50.0 \text{ in}^2$$

The formula to find the required section modulus to resist bending stress is

$$S = \frac{M}{f_b}$$
$$M = 15{,}000 \text{ ft-lb}$$
$$f_b = 1200 \text{ psi}$$

All units must be consistent.

Therefore,

$$S = \frac{(15,000 \text{ ft-lb}) \left(12 \, \frac{\text{in}}{\text{ft}} \right)}{1200 \, \frac{\text{lb}}{\text{in}^2}} = \frac{180,000 \text{ in-lb}}{1200 \, \frac{\text{lb}}{\text{in}^2}}$$

$$= 150.0 \text{ in}^3$$

The required area, A, then is 50.0 in², and the required section modulus, S, is 150.0 in³, allowing the beam to be sized from a table of properties.

43. **A**   The purpose of prestressing concrete is to permanently load concrete with stresses in the opposite direction to those caused by the eventual live and dead loads. By doing so, the entire cross section becomes effective in resisting those stresses. Prestressing concrete transfers the prestress from the steel to the concrete and therefore requires no end anchorages. Prestressing still does not eliminate concrete creep and shrinkage which reduce the prestressing force and should be considered in the design. Both pretensioning and posttensioning are the basic methods of prestressing concrete. Pretensioning involves prestressing the steel before the concrete is cast. Posttensioning involves prestressing the steel after the concrete is cast but before it is loaded.

44. **C**   In a solid sawn wood beam, the flexural stress is maximum at the top and bottom fibers, and it passes through the neutral axis where it is zero.

45. **C**   Standard engineering practice calls for the resisting moment of the dead load to be at least 1.5 times the overturning moment. The retaining wall in question is inadequate as designed. Therefore, additional dead load is needed to increase the resisting moment. Widening the footing of the retaining wall is the simplest solution for increasing the dead load and the resisting moment. Additional steel or a key in the footing would not affect the dead load or the resisting moment.

46. **B**   To find the reaction at R_2, the sum of the moments (which equals zero) around the point at R_1 needs to be calculated.

$$\left(600 \, \frac{\text{lb}}{\text{ft}} \right) (9 \text{ ft}) \left(10 \text{ ft} + \frac{9 \text{ ft}}{2} \right) + (400 \text{ lb})(22 \text{ ft})$$

$$+ (800 \text{ lb})(31 \text{ ft}) - R_2(25 \text{ ft}) = 0$$

$$R_2 = \frac{78,300 \text{ ft-lb} + 8800 \text{ ft-lb} + 24,800 \text{ ft-lb}}{25 \text{ ft}}$$

$$= 4476 \text{ lb}$$

47. **C**   To find the resultant force, the horizontal and vertical components of the diagonal force at 60° must be known. The horizontal component is

$$(2000 \text{ lb})(\cos 60°) = 1000 \text{ lb} \quad \text{[to the right]}$$

The vertical component is

$$(2000 \text{ lb})(\sin 60°) = 1732 \text{ lb} \quad \text{[downward]}$$

The horizontal components of both forces are summed.

$$2000 \text{ lb} + 1000 \text{ lb} = 3000 \text{ lb} \quad \text{[to the right]}$$

The only vertical component of both forces is 1732 lb downward. The two are then squared and added together and the resultant force diagonal is the square root of that result.

$$\sqrt{(3000 \text{ lb})^2 + (1732 \text{ lb})^2} = 3464 \text{ lb} \quad \begin{bmatrix} \text{acting to the} \\ \text{right on a} \\ \text{diagonal of 30°} \end{bmatrix}$$

48. **A**   Live load is the load calculated by a building's use and occupancy as determined from the building code. It does not include wind, seismic, or dead loads. There is no relationship between live load and dead load. Long-span structures are not required to be designed for higher live loads than conventional structures. Even if the live load is less than the dead load, the building code requires that the live load be considered in the building's structural design, and the building official cannot waive that requirement.

49. **B**   Several factors are used to determine the load bearing capacity of a wood column. The cross-sectional area of the column is used and is calculated by the dimensions of the column section. The ratio l/d is another factor, where l is the unbraced length of the column and d is the smallest dimension in the column plan. The modulus of elasticity is also considered, which is dictated by the species of wood used. The radius of gyration is used in determining the load bearing capacity of steel columns, not wood columns.

50. **D**   In composite design, concrete slabs are connected to steel beams. Because they are designed to act together, small steel beams can be used, resulting in a less expensive system when compared with conventional steel framing. Composite design uses shear connectors to develop the ultimate capacity of either the concrete or steel, whichever is less. Conventional steel framing can always be designed to carry the design loads, so this is not the reason for using composite design. The smaller steel beam sizes result in greater possibility for deflection, though, so deflection becomes a critical consideration in composite design.

Lateral Forces Division

Sample Examination

1. Wind forces are resisted by the following braced frame. The wind force is equal to 9 kips. What is the internal force in steel rod b?

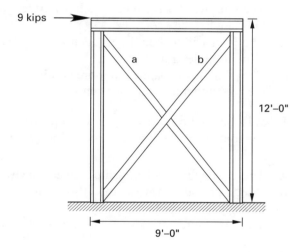

A. zero
B. 9.0 kips tension
C. 12.0 kips tension
D. 15.0 kips tension

2. In the design of a column footing, the calculations show that the shear in the footing exceeds the allowable limit. What change to the footing would solve the problem?

A. The thickness of the footing should be increased.
B. Reinforcing stirrups should be added.
C. Additional steel reinforcing should be provided.
D. The footing plan dimensions should be increased.

3. With regard to a low-rise building constructed with rigid frames, which of the following statements is incorrect?

A. Rigid frames are more rigid than braced frames of similar dimensions.
B. Steel or reinforced concrete may be used in rigid frames.
C. The joints of rigid frames are capable of resisting bending moment.
D. Rigid frames can resist both vertical and lateral loads.

4. Which of the following statements about damage from an earthquake is incorrect?

A. Slow, rocking motions of an earthquake are particularly damaging to tall buildings.
B. Surface ruptures cause more damage than ground shaking.
C. Heavy damage occurs where alluvial soils meet firmer soils.
D. Wood frame buildings perform relatively better than concrete or steel structures.

5. A one-story building is $50' \times 120'$. The 120-foot dimension is in the east-west direction. The building is constructed with plywood shear walls and diaphragms. Only the east, north, and south walls are shear walls. If a lateral force of 12 kips is applied to the building in the north-south direction, what is the rotational lateral shear force on the north and south shear walls?

A. 7.2 kips
B. 10.0 kips
C. 14.4 kips
D. 28.8 kips

6. Compared with an earthquake registering 5.0 on the Richter scale, an earthquake registering 7.0 is how much greater in magnitude?

   A. 40 percent greater
   B. 200 percent greater
   C. 320 percent greater
   D. 1000 percent greater

7. Which of the following structural systems are used to resist seismic forces in a building?

   I. box frames
   II. shear walls
   III. braced frames
   IV. moment-resisting frames
   V. space frames

   A. I, II, and III
   B. I, II, III, and IV
   C. II, III, and IV
   D. I, III, and V

8. If a building is designed according to the seismic requirements of the Uniform Building Code, which of the following statements is correct?

   A. The building will resist all forces due to an earthquake.
   B. The building will resist major earthquakes without collapse.
   C. The building will resist major earthquakes without damage.
   D. The building will resist ground movement, subsidence, and sliding due to major earthquakes.

9. According to Uniform Building Code requirements, which of the following are considered in the total lateral seismic design of a building element or component?

   I. geographic location
   II. directional orientation
   III. building occupancy
   IV. dead and live loads
   V. type of structural system

   A. I, II, III, and IV
   B. I, II, IV, and V
   C. I, III, and V
   D. II, III, IV, and V

10. Which of the following are considered in the wind pressure formula according to Uniform Building Code requirements?

    I. geographic location
    II. directional orientation
    III. building occupancy
    IV. building dead and live loads
    V. building height

    A. I, II, III, and IV
    B. I, II, IV, and V
    C. I, III, and V
    D. II, III, IV, and V

11. Which of the following statements regarding seismic joints that separate portions of a building is true?

    A. The width of the joint should equal the sum of the drifts in the two portions.
    B. The joint width should be 1 inch per 10 feet of building height.
    C. The joint width should be 1 inch per 100 feet of building length.
    D. The joint must separate the entire building from the roof down through the foundation.

12. What is the relationship between wind pressure in pounds per square foot and wind velocity in miles per hour?

    A. There is no direct relationship between the two.
    B. Wind pressure varies directly with wind velocity.
    C. Wind pressure varies with the square of wind velocity.
    D. Wind pressure varies inversely with wind velocity.

13. How is a building designed for lateral forces in seismic zone 4?

    A. designed for earthquake forces only
    B. designed for wind forces only
    C. designed for earthquake and wind forces acting together
    D. designed for earthquake and wind forces, but not both acting together

14. The following illustration shows a one-story rigid frame structure.

Which of the following diagrams correctly shows the stresses in the members? (C = compression and T = tension.)

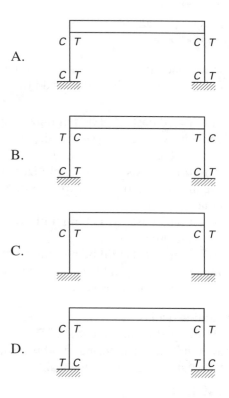

A.

B.

C.

D.

15. According to the Uniform Building Code, which statement regarding wind pressure for the design of a building is incorrect?

   A. Wind pressure acts either inward or outward on walls, but not in both directions at the same time.
   B. Wind pressure is greater at the corners than in the middle of a wall.
   C. Wind pressure is decreased when there are significant surface irregularities of the ground in the vicinity of the site.
   D. Wind pressure does not take into account the effect of tornadoes.

16. According to the Uniform Building Code, which statement regarding shear walls constructed with plywood sheathing is correct?

   A. The minimum width is 3 feet.
   B. The minimum width is dependent on the height of the wall.
   C. The minimum width equals the shear force divided by the allowable shear for the plywood.
   D. There is no minimum width.

17. What does the allowable shear in a blocked plywood diaphragm depend on?

   A. the length of framing members
   B. the direction of framing members
   C. the allowable stresses in the connection to the foundation
   D. the type and thickness of the plywood

18. Two buildings are constructed next to each other of nearly identical materials. Building A has a fundamental period of vibration calculated to be half a second. Building B's fundamental period of vibration is calculated to be one second. If all other factors are equal, which statement is correct?

   A. The buildings have equal seismic forces.
   B. Building A has a larger seismic force.
   C. Building A has a smaller seismic force.
   D. There is insufficient data to determine seismic force.

19. Which statement regarding seismic design is correct?

   A. A regular floor plan increases torsional stresses in a building during an earthquake.
   B. A building with upper-story shear walls and a "soft" ground floor will act independently in an earthquake.
   C. Nonstructural walls do not contribute to the seismic resistance of a building.
   D. Reinforced concrete columns often fail even with adequate ties.

20. The following building's center of rigidity is its center of mass. It resists seismic forces with horizontal diaphragms and vertical shear walls on the perimeter.

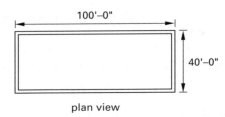

plan view

Which is the correct statement about the seismic design of the building?

A. Horizontal torsional moments equaling the story shear multiplied by 5 feet must be provided for, whether additive or deductive.
B. Horizontal torsional moments equaling the story shear multiplied by 5 feet must be provided for, but only if they are additive.
C. Horizontal torsional moments equaling the story shear multiplied by 2 feet must be provided for, but only if they are additive.
D. Horizontal torsional moments need not be provided for.

21. In a multistory building, how is the seismic force distributed to each floor and roof level?

A. equally at each level
B. in proportion to the weight of each individual floor
C. according to the ratio of $w_x h_x / \sum wh$
D. only when $K = 1.00$

22. What is the maximum diaphragm shear in the north-south direction for the following building with the force shown?

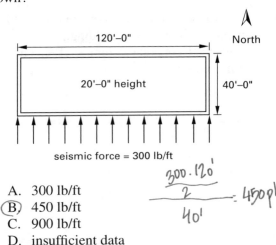

A. 300 lb/ft
B. 450 lb/ft
C. 900 lb/ft
D. insufficient data

23. What is the overturning moment on the east and west walls for the building in question 22? (Consider the weight of the walls negligible.)

A. 90,000 ft-lb
B. 180,000 ft-lb
C. 360,000 ft-lb
D. 720,000 ft-lb

24. What is the maximum diaphragm chord force in the north-south direction of the building in question 22?

A. 6750 pounds
B. 13,500 pounds
C. 27,000 pounds
D. 54,000 pounds

25. Providing lateral resistance of a building will add costs. Which statement about those additional costs is correct?

A. Additional costs will be minimized by using a separate structural system independent of the vertical load-carrying structure.
B. Additional costs will be minimized by exposing the system to visual expression, rather than concealing it.
C. Additional costs will be minimized by using a base-isolation system.
D. Additional costs will be minimized by designing the same vertical load-carrying members to resist lateral loads as well.

26. A retaining wall is 12 feet high. The earth it retains is properly drained behind the wall. The wall has no surcharge on it other than normal fluid pressure. What is the total pressure exerted on the wall?

A. 540 lb/ft
B. 1080 lb/ft
C. 2160 lb/ft
D. 4320 lb/ft

27. What is the ground surface location of an earthquake called?

A. fault
B. focus
C. hypocenter
D. epicenter

28. In seismic zone 1, when is a building required to be designed with a ductile moment-resisting space frame capable of resisting at least 25 percent of the total seismic force?

    A. when the building is over 160 feet in height
    B. when the building is over 320 feet in height
    C. when the building is rated as an essential occupancy
    D. it is not required

29. Which statement regarding box systems is correct?

    A. Box systems are as ductile as moment-resisting frames.
    B. Box systems may be used in any building.
    C. Box systems may not be made of steel.
    D. Box systems cannot resist axial forces.

30. The Uniform Building Code requires which of the following load combinations to be considered in lateral design?

    A. dead + floor live + wind (without roof live load)
    B. dead + floor live + roof live + wind
    C. dead + floor live + wind + snow load
    D. dead + floor live + snow load

31. For the following building plan, bents 1 are more rigid than bents 2. Which statement regarding the seismic resistance of each is correct?

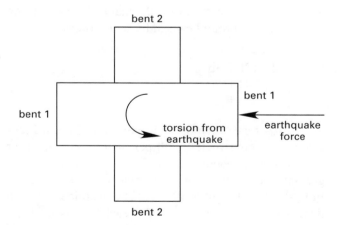

    A. Bents 1 resist all direct and torsional shear.
    B. Bents 2 resist all direct and torsional shear.
    C. Bents 1 resist direct shear; bents 2 resist torsional shear.
    D. Bents 1 resist torsional shear; bents 2 resist direct shear.

32. Which material may not be used to create a ductile moment-resisting space frame?

    A. reinforced concrete
    B. reinforced masonry
    C. precast concrete
    D. structural steel

33. What relationship does the fundamental period of vibration of a building have to its height?

    A. Period is directly proportional to height.
    B. Period is inversely proportional to height.
    C. Other factors determine whether period is directly or inversely proportional.
    D. No relationship exists between period and height.

34. Which building is an example of good seismic design?

    A. a 3-story rectangular wood-frame building with identical east and west shear walls and north and south shear walls that are twice as long and twice as thick as the east and west wall
    B. an 8-story U-shaped reinforced concrete-frame building with re-entrant corners at the intersections
    C. a 20-story rectangular steel-frame building with nonductile moment-resisting space frames on the perimeter and a concrete shear wall core
    D. a 40-story ductile moment-resisting space frame rigidly connected to a four-story concrete shear wall base

35. Which statements regarding wind and earthquake forces are correct?

    I. Both are based upon geographic location.
    II. The type of lateral resisting system determines the magnitude of both.
    III. The magnitude of both depends on the building height.
    IV. Vertical forces do not affect the design for either.
    V. The Uniform Building Code allows a 33 1/3 percent increase for allowable stresses for both.

    A. I, II, and III
    B. II, III, and V
    C. I, III, and V
    D. III, IV, and V

36. On what does the C factor in the seismic equation depend?

    A. the building's use or occupancy
    B. the building's geographic location
    C. the building's period of vibration
    D. the building's structural system

37. A 1-story building has a flat roof. Which statement is correct?

    A. The wind force is zero.
    B. The wind force acts downward.
    C. The wind force acts upward.
    D. The wind force acts upward or downward depending on the value of C_q.

38. The following shear wall is resisting a 10,000-pound wind load as shown. The wall also supports 6000-pound dead loads at each end. What is the uplift at point A?

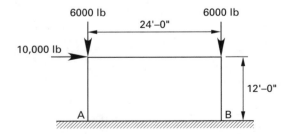

    A. zero
    B. 2000 pounds
    C. 4000 pounds
    D. 10,000 pounds

39. Rank the following lateral resisting systems in order of decreasing stiffness.

    I. shear wall
    II. braced frame
    III. moment-resisting frame

    A. I, II, III
    B. I, III, II
    C. II, III, I
    D. III, II, I

40. A $4' \times 12'$, 20-foot-high sign is to be designed for wind loads. If $C_e = 0.6, C_q = 1.7, q_s = 15$ pounds per square foot, and $I = 1.1$, what is the design wind pressure for the sign?

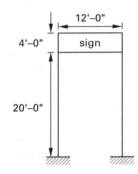

    A. 13.9 psf
    B. 15.3 psf
    C. 16.5 psf
    D. 16.8 psf

41. For the sign in question 40, what is the overturning moment at the ground caused by wind forces?

    A. 8064 ft-lb
    B. 16,128 ft-lb
    C. 17,741 ft-lb
    D. 19,354 ft-lb

42. A 10-story office building is located in San Francisco. It is constructed with perimeter concrete shear walls and suspended roof and floor slabs, including the ground floor. The floor plate measures $100' \times 100'$. Floor-to-floor height is 12 feet. The dead load of each floor is 1600 kips. The live load of each floor is 500 kips. The dead load of the roof is 1400 kips. Assume a C factor of 2.75. What is the total shear force at the base of the building?

    A. 2244 kips
    B. 2393 kips
    C. 3240 kips
    D. 3688 kips

43. In the following elevation of a two-story building, what member is used to connect the two shear walls?

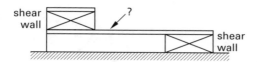

A. seismic joint
B. chord
C. diaphragm
D. collector

44. Which of the following statements is incorrect?

    I. Torsion occurs in a diaphragm when the center of mass is not coincident with the building centroid.

    II. Concrete diaphragms distribute lateral forces proportional to the rigidities of the vertical resisting members.

    III. Plywood diaphragms distribute lateral forces proportional to the tributary area of the vertical resisting members.

    IV. Plywood shear walls resist lateral forces in the wall plane.

A. I
B. I and II
C. II and III
D. III and IV

45. How must a building's individual components and their connections be designed for wind and seismic design?

A. Only the total lateral force resisting system must be designed, not individual components.
B. They must be designed for lesser forces than those used for designing the lateral force resisting system.
C. They must be designed for the same forces used for the lateral force resisting system.
D. They must be designed for greater forces than those used for designing the lateral force resisting system.

46. Which of the following is not considered in the design of retaining walls?

A. soil bearing pressure
B. shear
C. sliding
D. overturning moment

47. Which of the following building massings is the least effective in resisting overturning moment due to wind loads?

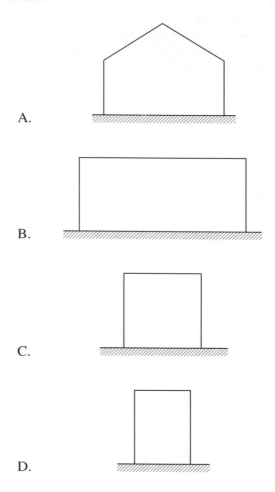

48. What was the major reason that so much damage occurred in the 1985 earthquake in Mexico City?

A. The city's building code was not current with earthquake standards.
B. Many structures were constructed poorly with substandard materials.
C. Many structures had periods of vibration coincident with that of the ground shaking.
D. The epicenter of the earthquake was very close to Mexico City.

49. A roof diaphragm constructed of which material will have the highest allowable shear value, assuming proper nailing?

    A. $1/2$-inch plywood sheathing
    B. 1-inch diagonal sheathing
    C. 1-inch straight sheathing
    D. 2-inch tongue-and-groove decking

50. What does the Modified Mercalli scale measure?

    A. the energy release of an earthquake
    B. the intensity of an earthquake
    C. the ground acceleration of an earthquake
    D. the period of vibration of an earthquake

Examination Answers with Explanations

1. D Steel rods can only act in tension to resist forces. Rod a is ineffective in resisting the wind load shown. All the braced frame resistance is taken by rod b. To find that force in rod b, isolate the upper right joint and calculate the formula $\sum H = 0$.

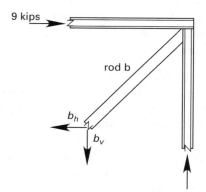

$$9 \text{ kips} - b_h = 0$$
$$b_h = 9 \text{ kips}$$

To find b_v, take the ratio of the vertical component to the horizontal component of the rod and multiply by b_h.

$$b_v = \left(\frac{12 \text{ ft}}{9 \text{ ft}}\right)(b_h) = (1.33)(9 \text{ kips})$$
$$= 12 \text{ kips}$$

The diagonal force in rod b then is the square root of the sum of the square roots of the vertical and horizontal components of the force.

$$\sqrt{b_h^2 + b_v^2} = \sqrt{(9 \text{ kips})^2 + (12 \text{ kips})^2}$$
$$\sqrt{(225 \text{ kips})^2} = 15.0 \text{ kips} \quad \text{[in tension]}$$

2. A The thickness of the footing should be increased. Two-way shear is usually critical in the design of column footings. Although stirrups could theoretically be used to take part of the shear stress, it is simpler and more efficient to thicken the footing itself. The amount of steel reinforcement is unrelated to shear stress and shear stress is virtually unaffected by the size of the footing in plan.

3. A A rigid frame, despite its name, is usually less rigid than a braced frame of similar dimensions. Rigid

frames are used in both high- and low-rise buildings and are constructed of either steel or reinforced concrete. A rigid frame is made up of beams and columns rigidly connected together so the joints resist bending moment. Both vertical and lateral (horizontal) loads (such as wind loads and seismic loads) are resisted very efficiently by rigid frames.

4. B Most earthquake damage is due to violent ground shaking over a period of time and not sudden surface faulting. Obviously, building over known faults should be avoided, but to minimize damage and danger to the public, it is more important to design structures to resist ground shaking. Tall buildings have long periods of vibration and tend to resonate with the same period as the slow, rocking earthquake motion. That motion changes patterns when traveling from soft alluvial soils to much firmer soils, creating abrupt changes in structural forces which cause excessive damage. Wood-frame buildings are well-designed for earthquake forces because of the flexible, organic nature of wood versus the rigidity and brittleness of steel and concrete.

5. C First, find the moment caused by the lateral force.

$$M = (12.0 \text{ kips})\left(\frac{120 \text{ ft}}{2}\right) = 720 \text{ kip-ft}$$
$$R_{\text{north}} = R_{\text{south}} = \text{rotational shear}$$
$$= \frac{720 \text{ kip-ft}}{50 \text{ ft}}$$
$$= 14.4 \text{ kips}$$

6. D The Richter scale is logarithmic. An increase in magnitude of each whole number (1.0, 2.0, 3.0, etc.) on the Richter scale represents an increase in magnitude of 32 times. For example, an earthquake measuring 7.0 will be 32 times greater than one measuring 6.0, which is 32 times greater than one measuring 5.0. 32 times 32 equals approximately 1000 percent, therefore the correct answer is choice D.

7. B All of the structural systems mentioned are used to resist seismic forces except a space frame (unless it is a moment-resisting space frame). A box frame is another term for a system using shear walls. Therefore, the correct answers are I, II, III, and IV.

8. B The seismic requirements of the Uniform Building Code provide buildings with the capability of resisting ground shaking due to an earthquake. The provisions do not address cases where faulting, subsidence, or earth sliding occur in the immediate vicinity of the building. They are intended to prevent buildings from collapsing and causing injury and/or death to the public. It is expected, however, that some damage, both structural and nonstructural, will occur, but will be repairable.

9. **C**   Per the Uniform Building Code, the total design lateral seismic force on a building element or component is expressed by the following formula.

$$F_p = ZIC_pW_p$$

The geographic location of the building is represented by Z, the seismic zone factor. I is the importance factor dependent on the building occupancy type. Numerical coefficient C_p is a horizontal force factor found in the Uniform Building Code. C_p is dependent on the structural elements and the nonstructural building components that are being designed for. The total dead load (without live load) of the building element or component is the W_p in the equation. Neither live load nor the building's directional orientation is considered in the formula.

10. **C**   Per the Uniform Building Code, the total wind pressure on a building is expressed by the formula

$$p = C_eC_qq_sI$$

The geographic location is represented by q_s, the stagnation pressure at a height of 30 feet. q_s is a function of the basic wind speed at the site location. C_e is the combination exposure, height, and gusting factor, which is a function of the building height. C_q is the coefficient of pressure for the portion of the building for which wind pressures are being designed. The final factor, I, is the importance factor that depends on the building occupancy and is higher for essential buildings than for other uses. Directional orientation and building loads are not factored into the formula for wind pressure.

11. **A**   Seismic joints are intended to prevent two adjacent portions of a building from hitting one another during an earthquake. To do this, the width of the joint should at least equal the sum of the drifts, or deflections, of the two portions. A width of 1 inch per 10 feet of height is only a rule of thumb and will not necessarily provide adequate isolation from the drift. Choice C is totally erroneous, as the drift depends on the seismic calculations, not on the building dimensions. It is also not necessary to separate the entire building down through the foundation.

12. **C**   Wind pressure varies with the square of the wind velocity. When wind velocity doubles, wind pressure increases four times.

13. **D**   The most seismically active zone is zone 4, with areas of California, Nevada, and Alaska having the highest risk of earthquake. The Uniform Building Code requires all buildings in any zone to be designed for either earthquake or wind forces. These forces, however, are considered to be acting independently and not at the same time. Whichever force is greater governs the lateral force design of the building.

14. **D**   In a rigid frame structure, the columns develop a point of zero moment (contraflexure) at approximately midheight. This is the point where compression (or tension) in the member reduces from maximum to zero and then continues to its opposite force. That is, maximum compression > zero > maximum tension, or vice versa. With the force applied as shown, the upper left part of the left column will be in compression and the upper right will be in tension. The opposite will be true for the upper parts of the right column. At midheight, these forces pass through zero and reverse. Therefore, the correct diagram of the stresses is shown in choice D.

15. **A**   Wind pressure creates both positive inward pressure and negative outward pressure on walls at the same time and must be considered as doing such in the design for the walls. Wind pressure is greater at the corners and other discontinuities of a wall than at the middle of a wall. Significant surface irregularities immediate to the site cause interference with wind, decreasing its velocity and therefore the design wind pressure. The Uniform Building Code takes into account the effects of hurricanes on wind pressure, but does not account for tornadoes, which often cause higher wind speeds.

16. **B**   The Uniform Buidling Code does not specify a minimum width for shear walls. Rather, the code specifies a maximum ratio of height to width of the shear wall, making the width directly dependent on the height of the wall. Even if calculations of the shear force divided by the allowable shear indicate a width less than the Uniform Building Code height-to-width ratios, the height-to-width ratio must be adhered to as the minimum width required.

17. **D**   The allowable shear in a blocked plywood diaphragm depends on the width, not the length, of framing members. As long as it is a blocked diaphragm, the direction of framing members does not affect the allowable shear. Diaphragms may be either walls, floors, or roofs. The stresses in the foundation do not directly affect the allowable shear in the diaphragm itself. The allowable shear is directly dependent on the type and thickness of the plywood used to make the diaphragm.

18. **B**   Seismic force is inversely related to a building's fundamental period of vibration. Therefore, the shorter the period, the higher the ground acceleration and the larger the seismic force. With longer periods, the ground acceleration is reduced, thereby reducing the seismic force. Since building A has the shorter period, Building A will have a larger seismic force.

19. **B**   A regular floor plan is preferred in seismic design. An irregular floor plan increases the torsional stresses due to an earthquake. A building with a "soft" ground floor and rigid shear walls above will act independently in an earthquake because the seismic resistance in the upper floors cannot be transferred properly to the foundation through the ground floor. This condition has been the cause of much earthquake damage in the past. Although nonstructural walls are assumed to have no calculated effect in resisting seismic forces, they do contribute to the overall seismic resistance of a building. In the past, column failures have been due to the inadequacy of the ties. With adequate ties, reinforced concrete columns rarely fail.

20. **B**   Horizontal torsional moment must be provided for in the seismic design. The minimum moment is the story shear multiplied by a 5 percent eccentricity of the maximum building dimension. In the example, 100 feet is the maximum dimension; therefore, multiplying by 5 percent equals 5 feet times the story shear. Negative torsional shears can be neglected, so the correct answer is choice B.

21. **C**   The seismic force is distributed to each level x according to the formula

$$F_x = \frac{(V - F_t)(w_x h_x)}{\sum wh}$$

w_x = dead load of each level x, h_x = height of level x above the base, and $\sum wh$ = the summation of the wh quantities for each level. If the weight of each story is equal, the lateral forces of the total base shear V are distributed in the form of an inverted triangle with the maximum force at the top and zero at the base.

22. **B**   The diaphragm actually acts like a horizontal beam. The reactions at the east and west end walls equal $F/2$.

$$\frac{F}{2} = \frac{wL}{2} = \frac{\left(300\ \dfrac{\text{lb}}{\text{ft}}\right)(120\ \text{ft})}{2}$$
$$= 18{,}000\ \text{lb}$$

To find the diaphragm shear, divide the reaction force by the length of the wall.

$$v = \frac{18{,}000\ \text{lb}}{40\ \text{ft}} = 450\ \text{lb/ft}$$

23. **C**   From the calculations in the answer to question 22, the horizontal force applied to each of the end walls is known to be 18,000 pounds. To find the overturning moment, multiply this force by the height of the wall.

$$M = (18{,}000\ \text{lb})(20\ \text{ft}) = 360{,}000\ \text{ft-lb}$$

24. **B**   Because the diaphragm acts like a horizontal beam, its chord force is like the force in a beam flange. The maximum moment in the diaphragm beam is

$$M = \frac{wL^2}{8} = \frac{\left(300\ \dfrac{\text{lb}}{\text{ft}}\right)(120\ \text{ft})^2}{8}$$
$$= 540{,}000\ \text{ft-lb}$$

The maximum chord force is

$$T = C = \frac{M}{d}$$
$$d = 40\ \text{ft}$$
$$C = \frac{540{,}000\ \text{ft-lb}}{40\ \text{ft}} = 13{,}500\ \text{lb}$$

25. **D**   In general, a separate structural system for seismic forces (independent of the vertical load-carrying system) is inefficient and uneconomical and will not minimize the additional costs. The visual expression of an exposed system is usually based on aesthetics, not economy, as it could be very expensive to detail such a system in order to expose it for appearance. Base isolation systems are very sophisticated and very expensive, and they will not minimize additional costs. The correct method to minimize those additional costs is to design the vertical load-carrying system to resist lateral loads as well.

26. **C**   Walls retaining drained earth are designed for an equivalent fluid pressure of 30 pounds per cubic foot, plus any surcharge (which is zero in the question).

Therefore, the pressure at the bottom of a 12-foot wall equals the height times the fluid pressure.

$$(12\,\text{ft})\left(30\,\frac{\text{lb}}{\text{ft}^3}\right) = 360\,\text{lb/ft}^2\ \ (\text{psf})$$

The total pressure on the wall equals the average pressure on the wall multiplied by the height of the wall itself.

$$\frac{\left(360\,\frac{\text{lb}}{\text{ft}^2}\right)(12\,\text{ft})}{2} = 2160\,\text{lb/ft}$$

27. **D** The fault is the boundary between adjacent tectonic plates and occurs deep in the earth's crust. The location where the plate slippage first begins in the crust is called the focus or hypocenter. The location of the projection of the focus on the ground surface is known as the epicenter.

28. **D** A ductile moment-resisting space frame is not required for a building in seismic zone 1, since zone 1 denotes low risk of seismic activity. In zones 3 and 4, buildings over 160 feet in height must be designed with ductile moment-resisting space frames.

29. **B** Box systems use shear walls and/or braced frames to form a "box" used to resist lateral forces. They can be constructed with reinforced masonry, reinforced concrete, steel, or wood. Any building can utilize a box system, but in zones 3 and 4, buildings over 160 feet in height must use a ductile moment-resisting space frame in addition to the box system. Box systems resist lateral loads by both shear and axial forces.

30. **A** For lateral design, the Uniform Building Code requires that structural members be designed to resist the combination of dead plus floor live plus wind, without the roof live load. Another combination allowed by the Uniform Building Code is dead plus floor live plus wind plus either half the snow load, or half the wind load. Snow loads and wind loads do not have to be considered at their full values due to the small probability of their being maximum at the same time.

31. **C** Bents 1, because they are stiffer than bents 2, will resist most of the direct shear due to an earthquake in the direction shown. Bents 2, because they are further from the center of the building where the earthquake is acting, will resist most of the shear from torsion.

32. **B** Ductile moment-resisting space frames are moment-resisting frames made of structural steel or reinforced concrete. To be ductile they must have the capability to absorb large amounts of energy in the inelastic range without failure or appreciable deformity.

Most such frames constructed with concrete are of cast-in-place concrete. Precast concrete with reinforcement can be used for beams and columns that are joined at points of minimum moment. Reinforced masonry is not acceptable for ductile moment-resisting space frames.

33. **A** The value of T, the fundamental period of vibration of a structure, is calculated from the following formula.

$$T = \frac{0.05h}{\sqrt{D}}$$

h is the height, and D is the building dimension parallel to the forces being applied. As the height increases, the period increases. Therefore, the period of vibration is directly proportional to the building's height.

34. **C** The building in choice A is not a good example due to its lack of symmetry in its structural rigidity. The building has a regular rectangular floor plan with the length twice the width. With the north and south shear walls twice the length of the east and west, their thickness should be half as much as the east and west walls to provide a rigid structure that is symmetrical. The building in choice B is also not a good example. In irregular buildings with separate wings (such as a U-shape) the re-entrant corners are weak points for seismic forces and should be avoided by providing seismic joints to separate the various portions of the building at these corners. The building in choice C is a good example of proper seismic design. It is a typical structure with a service core of concrete shear walls with moment-resisting space frames to resist vertical loads at the perimeter. Finally, the building in choice D is also not a good example. When buildings have different structural systems that behave differently under lateral loads, the structural systems should not be rigidly connected to each other. This is typically avoided by using a seismic joint to avoid potential damage.

35. **C** As shown on maps in the Uniform Building Code, both wind and earthquake forces are based on geographic locations. The type of lateral resisting system is only factored into the formula for earthquake forces, not for wind. The magnitude of both forces depends on the height of the building. As building height increases, so do wind forces; also dead load of the building increases, which increases the earthquake forces. Vertical loads do not affect wind forces, but they do affect earthquake forces, again because the vertical loads (both dead and live) of the building factor into the seismic equation. Finally, the Uniform Building Code permits a 33 1/3% increase in allowable stresses for both wind and earthquake forces.

36. C Following is the seismic equation.

$$V = \left(\frac{ZIC}{R_w}\right) W$$

The Z factor is a coefficient of the geographic location, which determines the seismic zone 0–4 in which the building is located. The I factor is the importance factor, which is dependent upon the building's use or occupancy. C is a numerical coefficient which accounts for the building's acceleration—the dynamic response to ground motion caused by an earthquake. The formula for C involves the square root of the period of vibration and is therefore dependent upon it. The building's structural system is considered by the R_w numerical coefficient, which is a tabular value given in the Uniform Building Code based upon the structural system used. The total seismic dead load of the building is represented by the W factor.

37. C According to the Uniform Building Code, a roof with less than 9:12 pitch has a wind force coefficient C_q of 1.1 acting "outward." Outward means upward, therefore choice C is correct.

38. A To solve for uplift at point A, the moments around point B must be found.

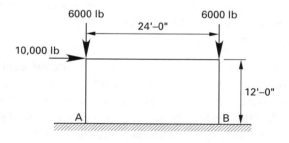

$$\text{overturning moment} = (10,000 \text{ lb})(12 \text{ ft})$$
$$= 120,000 \text{ ft-lb} \quad \begin{bmatrix} \text{due to the} \\ \text{wind load} \end{bmatrix}$$

$$\text{resisting moment} = (6000 \text{ lb})(24 \text{ ft})$$
$$= 144,000 \text{ ft-lb} \quad \begin{bmatrix} \text{due to the dead} \\ \text{load at point A} \end{bmatrix}$$

The dead load at point B creates no moment as it passes through point B. Since the 144,000 ft-lb resisting moment exceeds the 120,000 ft-lb overturning moment, there will be zero uplift.

39. A Resistance to deflection and deformation is known as stiffness. The shear wall is the stiffest when under lateral loads, whereas the moment-resisting frame is the most flexible and will deflect the most. The braced frame is between the two in terms of stiffness. Therefore, ranking them in order of decreasing stiffness, shear wall would be first, braced frame second, and moment-resisting frame third.

40. D The formula for wind pressure is

$$p = C_e C_q q_s I$$
$$= (0.6)(1.7)(15 \text{ psf})(1.1)$$
$$= 16.83 \text{ psf}$$

41. C From the calculations in the answer to question 40, the design wind pressure is 16.8 pounds per square foot. Multiplying this by the area of the sign gives total wind pressure.

$$\left(16.8 \, \frac{\text{lb}}{\text{ft}^2}\right)(4 \text{ ft})(12 \text{ ft}) = 806.4 \text{ lb}$$

This pressure acts at the center of the sign, that is 22 ft (20 ft + 4 ft/2) above the ground. The overturning moment due to the wind force is found by multiplying the total force by the height above ground.

$$M = (806.4 \text{ lb})(22 \text{ ft}) = 17,740.8 \text{ ft-lb}$$

42. B The formula for lateral base shear is

$$V = \left(\frac{ZIC}{R_w}\right) W$$

San Francisco is in zone 4, so $Z = 0.40$. An office building is not an essential facility, so $I = 1.00$. To find the C factor,

$$C = \frac{1.25 \, S}{T^{2/3}}$$

The period of vibration, T, must be calculated from

$$T = C_t (h_n)^{3/4}$$

As these calculations are overly complicated for the exam, the maximum value of 2.75 will be used. (2.75 is the maximum value required by the building code without regard to soil type or period of vibration.) From the Uniform Building Code, $R_w = 8$ for concrete shear walls. W, the total dead weight (not including live loads) of the building, must then be found.

$$W = 10 \text{ floors} + \text{roof} = (10)(1600 \text{ kips}) + 1400 \text{ kips}$$
$$= 17,400 \text{ kips}$$

Solving for V,

$$V = \left(\frac{ZIC}{R_w}\right) W$$

$$= \left[\frac{(0.40)(1.00)(2.75)}{8}\right](17,400\,\text{kips})$$

$$= (0.1375)(17,400\,\text{kips})$$

$$= 2392.5\,\text{kips} \quad \begin{bmatrix} \text{total shear at the} \\ \text{base of the building} \end{bmatrix}$$

43. D To transfer seismic loads from the offsetting shear walls of the building in question, a "collector" or "drag" or "strut" is used. These members may be structural in other capacities as well, such as beams, ledgers, plates, horizontal steel, etc.

44. A All of the statements are true except for I. When the center of mass is also the center of rigidity, lateral forces cannot create rotation or torsion in the diaphragm. The center of rigidity is unrelated to the building's centroid.

45. D Damage from wind or earthquake forces often occurs to individual elements and their connections, rather than to the building's lateral resisting system. Consequently, both structural and nonstructural components and connections have specific design requirements to resist damage from both forces. The forces used for the design of these elements are usually greater than those used for the design of the building's lateral resisting system.

46. B All of the factors are used in the design of retaining walls except for shear. To resist the soil pressure, the wall footing must take into account the allowable soil bearing pressure to resist the tendency of the wall to overturn. The lateral pressure from the soil being retained (and the equivalent fluid pressure) causes the wall to slide and overturn.

47. D Wind forces cause overturning moment in buildings in the same way that earthquake forces do. The overturning moment is directly proportional to a building's height-to-width ratio. Short or squat buildings tend to have smaller overturning moments than taller or narrower buildings. Since the building shown in choice D has the greatest height-to-width ratio, it will have the highest overturning moment and will be least effective in resisting the overturning moment due to wind forces.

48. C The 1985 Mexico City earthquake was the worst ever to occur in North America in terms of human casualties and property damage. The earthquake registered 8.1 on the Richter scale. The epicenter was actually on the coast, over 200 miles from Mexico City. The city's building code was current with earthquake standards and was considered excellent. Most of the damaged buildings were properly designed and constructed with proper seismic engineering per current practices. Because Mexico City was constructed on an ancient lake bed, the period of vibration of the ground shaking was long, about two seconds, which coincided with the period of vibration of most of the buildings that collapsed or were severely damaged. The coincidence of the two periods greatly amplified the ground waves, causing severe damage and collapse.

49. A $\frac{1}{2}$-inch plywood sheathing with proper nailing has a higher allowable shear value than any other type of wood diaphragm, whether used for roof, floor, or wall diaphragms.

50. B Two different scales are used to measure earthquakes. The Richter scale uses scientific instruments to measure the total energy released in an earthquake. The Modified Mercalli scale measures the intensity of an earthquake by its observed effects on buildings and perceived reactions of people affected.

Mechanical and Electrical Systems Division

Sample Examination

1. In heating and cooling system calculations, what is a degree day?

    A. the heat content of a fossil fuel
    B. the average temperature below 65°F
    C. the solar heat gain expressed in degrees
    D. the outside design temperature

2. A residential bathroom has no window to provide natural ventilation. The room size is $5' \times 10' \times 8'$. What is the minimum acceptable capacity of a ventilation fan in cubic feet per minute?

    A. 40 cfm
    B. 400 cfm
    C. 2000 cfm
    D. insufficient data

3. A drain pipe runs horizontally from a toilet to a soil stack with a slope of ¼ inch per foot. What is the difference in elevation between each end of a 12-foot-long pipe run?

    A. 0.25 inches
    B. 1.5 inches
    C. 3.0 inches
    D. 0.3 feet

4. If the absolute humidity of air is increased without a change in the dry bulb temperature, what will happen?

    A. Relative humidity will decrease.
    B. The dew point will fall.
    C. Wet bulb temperature will decrease.
    D. Enthalpy will increase.

5. A room in a house is calculated to have a heat loss of 6000 BTU per hour for forced air heating. Supply duct air temperature is 130°F dry bulb, and 80°F wet bulb. The room is designed to have a dry bulb temperature of 72°F. What air flow (in cubic feet per minute) will be required?

    A. 95 cfm
    B. 105 cfm
    C. 110 cfm
    D. 120 cfm

6. Which type of fire extinguisher would you not want to use for a Class C fire?

    A. carbon dioxide
    B. dry powder
    C. soda acid
    D. Halon

7. Which of the following statements is false?

    A. Surface runoff water is usually softer than well water.
    B. Surface runoff water is likely to have a lower carbon dioxide content than well water.
    C. Well water usually has a lower level of suspended solids than surface runoff water.
    D. Well water tends to be purer than surface runoff water.

8. Which of the following heat values is correct?

    A. 14,600 BTU/lb of coal
    B. 1000 BTU/kWh of electricity
    C. 3000 BTU/ft³ of natural gas
    D. 14,000 BTU/gal of heavy fuel oil

9. A 12-inch-diameter sewer line has an invert elevation of 101.5 feet at the center of a parking lot. What is the centerline elevation of the pipe at that location?

    A. 101.0 feet
    B. 101.5 feet
    C. 102.0 feet
    D. 102.5 feet

10. An art gallery space, $25' \times 60' \times 18'$ is to have air changed five times per hour. What air flow (in cubic feet per minute) is required?

    A. 1000 cfm
    B. 2250 cfm
    C. 5400 cfm
    D. 7500 cfm

11. What unit of measure is used to specify light reflectance?

    A. candelas
    B. footlamberts
    C. footcandles
    D. lumens per watt

12. Which statement is incorrect?

    A. A dry standpipe does not need a backup water connection.
    B. A fire alarm system should have both audible and visible alarms.
    C. A POC detector detects both visible and invisible gases.
    D. In the event of sprinkler actuation, a dry standpipe system causes less water damage than a wet standpipe system.

13. How is light generated in the glass chamber of an HPS lamp?

    A. by a high intensity arc
    B. by halogen vapor
    C. by a tungsten filament
    D. by fluorescent phosphor

14. Which statement regarding sound is correct?

    A. The velocity of sound traveling in steel is less than 1130 feet per second.
    B. The ear is more sensitive to sound at 300 Hz than 1000 Hz.
    C. 25 dB plus 25 dB equals 50 dB.
    D. Sound intensity increases by 6 dB when the distance to the source is halved.

15. A proposed residence is to be served by a highly acidic water supply. How does this influence the plumbing systems?

    A. Black iron pipe can be used because it contains no zinc.
    B. Copper tubing cannot be used because it contains zinc.
    C. Copper tubing can be used because acid will not affect it.
    D. Galvanized steel should be used to protect the steel pipe.

16. What is the maximum noise level that OSHA regulations will permit workers to be exposed to when they work an 8-hour shift?

    A. 80 dB
    B. 90 dB
    C. 100 dB
    D. 110 dB

17. To prevent backflow in a plumbing line, which would be used?

    A. an air gap
    B. a surge arrester
    C. a spring-loaded check valve
    D. a pressure-relief valve

18. The lighting design of a banquet room utilizes fluorescent fixtures with four 40-watt lamps with 3200 lumens per lamp. The room dimensions are $80' \times 160'$ with a 16-ft-high ceiling. The maintenance factor is 0.8, and the coefficient of utilization is 0.6. If 120 footcandles are desired, how many fixtures are needed?

    A. 100 fixtures
    B. 250 fixtures
    C. 333 fixtures
    D. 500 fixtures

19. Which is true of a return line for a circulating hot water system?

    A. It has the same pipe size as the outgoing hot water supply.
    B. It connects to the water heater discharge pipe.
    C. It connects to the bottom of the storage tank.
    D. It connects to the top of the storage tank.

20. If a 200 kVA transformer is rated at 480–120/240 V, what is the rated current of the primary at full load?

    A. 138 A
    B. 240 A
    C. 417 A
    D. 481 A

21. Which of the following statements about heat pumps is false?

    A. They work only within certain temperature ranges.
    B. They work in essentially the same manner as air conditioning units.
    C. They cannot provide more heat energy than the energy required to run the pumps.
    D. They are frequently used in connection with a recirculating heat sink.

22. The peak cooling load for an office building is calculated to be 120,000 BTU per hour. In designing the HVAC system, how many tons of air conditioning will be needed?

    A. 10 tons
    B. 12 tons
    C. 20 tons
    D. 60 tons

23. An HVAC rooftop unit produces 60 dB of sound. If two of these units are used together in the system, what is their combined sound level?

    A. 57 dB
    B. 60 dB
    C. 63 dB
    D. 120 dB

24. Which of the following are not fire extinguishing agents?

    I. metal halide
    II. carbon dioxide
    III. Freon
    IV. Halon

    A. I and II
    B. I and III
    C. II and IV
    D. III and IV

25. Certain plumbing systems utilize a leaching field. What is its main purpose?

    A. A leaching field allows sewage that is free of solid waste to seep into the ground.
    B. A leaching field removes gray water before it enters the public sewage system.
    C. A leaching field stores sanitary waste until it is pumped out and removed.
    D. A leaching field stores storm water runoff until it can seep into the ground.

26. For a passive solar design, which of the following statements is not usually true?

    A. It relies on an active backup mechanical system.
    B. It is cheaper to build than a conventional building.
    C. It allows solar radiation into the building during winter.
    D. It stores heat in thermal mass materials.

27. What is the primary function of a trap in a plumbing system?

    A. It provides a cleanout when drains become clogged.
    B. It catches grease before it clogs the drain.
    C. It catches small items and objects that are accidentally dropped down the drain so they can be retrieved.
    D. It keeps sewer gas from entering the building.

28. An existing warehouse is to be converted into loft apartments. There is a working steam heat system but no air conditioning. To provide HVAC to the units, which is the best system to choose?

    A. a multizone system, which requires less space than other systems and provides HVAC for different zones
    B. a double duct forced air system, which provides heating and cooling to each unit and is separately controlled from each unit
    C. a heat pump system, which provides heating and cooling for each unit without the addition of ductwork
    D. a variable air volume (VAV) system, which is the most efficient at allowing a unit to be heated while an adjacent unit is cooled

29. What is the purpose of a catch basin?

    A. It collects the water under a plumbing fixture.
    B. It traps solid objects to prevent clogging a sewer line.
    C. It collects surface runoff and admits it into a storm drain.
    D. It collects overflow and holds it until it can be drained.

30. A space in a building measures $30' \times 60'$ with a 15-foot-high ceiling. The walls, floor, and ceiling are of the same material, with a coefficient of absorption of 0.04 sabins. What is the total absorptivity of the space?

    A. 180 sabins
    B. 252 sabins
    C. 504 sabins
    D. 1080 sabins

31. An electrical appliance with a resistance of 6 ohms is connected to a 120-volt duplex outlet. What is the current flow when the appliance is operating?

    A. 0.2 A
    B. 6.0 A
    C. 7.2 A
    D. 20.0 A

32. In a commercial building, the electrical conduit system is to be embedded in the concrete slab. Which of the following is unacceptable?

    A. IMC conduit
    B. EMT conduit
    C. flex conduit
    D. rigid conduit

33. The fire protection system for a school building requires a wet standpipe system. Within what distance of a hose outlet must every point on each floor be?

    A. 75 feet
    B. 100 feet
    C. 130 feet
    D. 150 feet

34. Which of the following lamps is the most efficient, that is, provides the most lumens per watt?

    A. high pressure sodium
    B. metal halide
    C. mercury vapor
    D. ultralume fluorescent

35. Which of the following statements concerning glare in a lighting system is true?

    I. Glare is always a very high illumination.
    II. Glare is always an extreme contrast in brightness.
    III. Glare is always a reflection.

    A. I only
    B. II only
    C. III only
    D. I, II, and III

36. What is the major advantage to using low voltage incandescent lamps?

    A. They can operate at very high temperatures.
    B. They last much longer than standard incandescents.
    C. They are much brighter for a given wattage.
    D. They focus and aim the light more accurately.

37. In a three-phase transformer, the voltage between the neutral of the wye and the endpoint is 120 volts. What is the voltage between the endpoints?

    A. 120 V
    B. 208 V
    C. 240 V
    D. 277 V

38. What is the reason that a sanitary sewage system is separate from the storm drainage system?

    I. Sanitary waste systems are pressurized; a storm drainage system is not.
    II. Storm drainage is more polluted than sanitary sewage.
    III. Storm drainage flows at high volume and is not treatable by sewage treatment plants.

    A. I only
    B. II only
    C. III only
    D. I and III

39. An electrical circuit has three parallel paths, one with a resistance of 4 ohms and two with a resistance of 8 ohms. What is the total net resistance of the circuit?

    A. $0.5 \, \Omega$
    B. $0.625 \, \Omega$
    C. $2.0 \, \Omega$
    D. $12.0 \, \Omega$

40. The total thermal resistance of an exterior building wall is 25.3-hr-ft^2-°F/BTU. What is the U-value of the wall when the ambient air temperature is 80°F?

  - A. 0.04 BTU/hr-ft^2-°F
  - B. 0.4 BTU/hr-ft^2-°F
  - C. 3.16 BTU/hr-ft^2-°F
  - D. 20.24 BTU/hr-ft^2-°F

41. Which of the following are integral parts in the refrigeration cycle of an air conditioning system?

  - I. evaporator coil
  - II. cooling tower
  - III. Freon
  - IV. expansion valve
  - V. compressor

  - A. I, II, and III
  - B. I, III, and IV
  - C. I, II, III, and V
  - D. I, II, III, IV, and V

42. A ceiling downlight in a room 11 feet high has an output of 4000 candelas. The floor material has a reflectance of 60 percent. What is the brightness on the floor directly below the light?

  - A. 16.7 footcandles
  - B. 19.8 footlamberts
  - C. 30.3 footlamberts
  - D. 33.1 footcandles

43. Which is the best shape for a supply duct in a forced air heating system, assuming space is not a problem and all have equal capacities?

  - A. round
  - B. square
  - C. rectangular
  - D. any of the above

44. A building is 8 stories high with a floor-to-floor height of 12 feet. A hose bibb on the rooftop requires 30 pounds per square inch pressure to operate properly. To provide adequate pressure to that fixture, what is the minimum water pressure necessary at the street water main? (Assume a loss of 10 pounds per square inch due to friction from the street to the building.)

  - A. 40 psi
  - B. 55 psi
  - C. 82 psi
  - D. 98 psi

45. The effects of conduction and time lag are two factors included in cooling load temperature differential (CLTD). What is the other factor included in CLTD?

  - A. absorptivity
  - B. transmissivity
  - C. radiation
  - D. convection

46. In a fluid medium, what is the thermal transfer process taking place known as?

  - A. transmissivity
  - B. radiation
  - C. conduction
  - D. convection

47. Which is the best mechanical system to use to provide separate utility bills for each zone in a building?

  - A. a heat pump system
  - B. a variable air volume system
  - C. a fan coil system
  - D. a multizone system

48. Which of the following statements is true for a ground fault interrupter (GFI)?

  - I. It can completely disconnect a circuit.
  - II. It protects against short circuits.
  - III. It can be activated even when nothing in the circuit is switched on.

  - A. I and II only
  - B. I and III only
  - C. II and III only
  - D. I, II, and III

49. What type of electric motor is used for elevators?

  - A. a three-phase induction motor
  - B. a single-phase a-c motor
  - C. a d-c motor
  - D. a universal motor

50. What type of material allows light to be transmitted through it without also transmitting the image on the far side?

  - A. reflective
  - B. translucent
  - C. opaque
  - D. transparent

Examination Answers with Explanations

1. B Degree day is a statistic that accumulates the number of days having an average temperature below 65°F and the amount by which they are below 65°F. The formula for degree day is

$$\left[65°F - \left(\begin{array}{c}\text{average temperature}\\\text{for one day}\end{array}\right)\right]\left(\begin{array}{c}\text{number of days}\\\text{in consideration}\end{array}\right)$$

The main use of this statistic is for calculating seasonal heating and cooling loads and for sizing HVAC equipment to compensate for those loads.

2. A The Uniform Building Code requires a minimum of five air changes per hour for residential bathrooms in group R occupancy. Therefore,

$$\dfrac{\left(\begin{array}{c}\text{room}\\\text{volume}\end{array}\right)\left(\begin{array}{c}\text{changes}\\\text{per hour}\end{array}\right)}{60\,\dfrac{\text{min}}{\text{hr}}} = \dfrac{(10\text{ ft})(5\text{ ft})(8\text{ ft})\left(\dfrac{5\text{ changes}}{\text{hr}}\right)}{60\,\dfrac{\text{min}}{\text{hr}}}$$

$$= \dfrac{2000\text{ ft}^3}{60\,\dfrac{\text{min}}{\text{hr}}}$$

$$= 33.33\text{ ft}^3/\text{min (cfm)}$$

Therefore, 40 cubic feet per minute is the minimum acceptable.

3. C The difference in elevation is found by multiplying the length of run by the slope of run (in like units).

$$\left(0.25\,\dfrac{\text{in}}{\text{ft}}\right)(12\text{ ft}) = 3.0\text{ in}$$

4. D An increase in absolute humidity without a change in the dry bulb temperature will cause all of the listed factors to rise, not decrease.

5. A The 80°F wet bulb temperature is irrelevant because the problem involves heating only, not cooling. The formula for air flow, Q, in cubic feet per minute is

$$Q = \dfrac{q_{total}}{(1.08)(\Delta T)} = \dfrac{6000\,\dfrac{\text{BTU}}{\text{hr}}}{\left(1.08\,\dfrac{\dfrac{\text{BTU}}{\text{hr}}}{\dfrac{\text{ft}^3}{\text{min}}\text{-}°F}\right)(130°F - 72°F)}$$

$$= \dfrac{6000\,\dfrac{\text{BTU}}{\text{hr}}}{\left(1.08\,\dfrac{\dfrac{\text{BTU}}{\text{hr}}}{\dfrac{\text{ft}^3}{\text{min}}\text{-}°F}\right)(58°F)}$$

$$= 96\text{ ft}^3/\text{min (cfm)}$$

Note: For heating, the temperature differential is between the dry bulb and the design temperature. For cooling, the wet bulb temperature is used for the differential.

6. C A Class C fire is an electrical fire. All of the materials listed could be used with the exception of soda acid, which may cause electrical shock.

7. B Although all natural water absorbs some carbon dioxide through the atmosphere, well water loses most of it through chemical reaction with minerals in the earth. Well water dissolves more magnesium and calcium compounds out of the earth because of its longer contact, so it will be harder than surface runoff. With the earth acting as a filter, well water becomes purer than surface runoff and contains less suspended solids.

8. A Coal will yield 14,600 BTU per pound. Electricity yields 3413 BTU per kilowatt-hour, natural gas yields 1040 BTU per cubic foot, and heavy fuel oil yields about 140,000 BTU per gallon.

9. C The inside surface of the bottom of the pipe is known as the invert elevation. Since the pipe is 12 inches in diameter, the centerline would be 6 inches higher or 102.0 feet.

10. B Because air changes are required five times per hour, the total volume of the space must be exchanged every 12 minutes. The formula is

$$\dfrac{(25\text{ ft})(60\text{ ft})(18\text{ ft})}{12\text{ min}} = 2250\text{ ft}^3/\text{min (cfm)}$$

11. B Footlamberts are units of measure for the number of lumens reflected from a square foot of surface area. Candelas are units of measure for the intensity or brightness of a light source (formerly called a candle). Footcandles are units of measure for the number of lumens striking a square foot of surface area. Finally, lumens per watt is a measure of the light output of a lamp versus the electrical input, which determines the lamp's efficiency.

12. D Sprinklers cause damage when activated; standpipe systems do not and are used only to supply water to the sprinkler system. A dry standpipe system never has any water connected to it unless the fire department connects its equipment via the siamese connection. Accessibility requirements mandate that a fire alarm system must warn both deaf and blind people; therefore, visible and audible alarm systems are required. A POC (products of combustion) smoke detector is activated by both visible and invisible gases.

13. **A** High pressure sodium (HPS) lamps are high intensity discharge (HID) lamps. They have electrodes within a quartz glass chamber filled with sodium, mercury, and xenon. An intense arc between the electrodes charges the gases and emits a brilliant light. The other elements listed are found in different types of lamps, not HID types.

14. **D** Sound travels more rapidly in solids than in air. The sensitivity of the human ear decreases above and below 3000 Hz. Doubling the sound increases the intensity by only about 3 dB. Choice D is an example of the inverse square law. As the distance is halved, the sound increases by four times, resulting in a 6 dB (3 dB + 3 dB) gain.

15. **C** Copper contains no zinc and is therefore not subject to dezincification caused by acidic water. Galvanizing is the application of a layer of pure zinc over steel to protect the steel, but acid will attack the zinc and then the steel. Black iron has only a paint coating, which offers less protection from acid than galvanizing does for steel.

16. **B** According to OSHA regulations, the maximum noise level is 90 dB for workers without other protection. Noise exceeding this level requires limits on exposure time, ear protectors, or other special precautions.

17. **A** An air gap is the only correct method of backflow prevention among those listed. A vacuum breaker could also be used. A surge arrester controls water hammer, not backflow. A spring-loaded check valve is not acceptable as a backflow preventer. A pressure-relief valve controls only built-up pressure, not backflow.

18. **B** The ceiling height is irrelevant since the illumination in footcandles is given. The formula is

$$N = \frac{(area)(footcandles)}{\left(\dfrac{lumens}{lamp}\right)\left(\dfrac{lamps}{fixture}\right)\left(\begin{array}{c}maintenance\\factor\end{array}\right)\left(\begin{array}{c}coefficient\\of\ utilization\end{array}\right)}$$

$$= \frac{(80\ ft)(160\ ft)(120\ footcandles)}{(3200)(4)(0.8)(0.6)}$$

$$= 250\ fixtures$$

19. **C** The return water in a circulating system will be a little cooler than that in the hot water storage tank.

If it were connected to the top, it would mix and cool the water already heated and stored at the top. Cooler water settles to the bottom of the tank so the return line should connect at the bottom. Because the water heater is connected to the storage tank at the tops of both, the return line should not be connected at the top of either tank. The return pipe does not need to be the same size as the supply pipe to the fixtures; it needs to be only large enough to provide the slow circulation required by the system itself.

20. **B** If a transformer is rated 480–120/240 V, the primary is 480 volts and the secondary is 240 volts, line to line. With 120/240 V on the secondary, the transformer has to be three-phase. For a three-phase transformer, the line current formula is

$$I = \frac{(transformer\ rating\ in\ kVA)\left(1000\ \dfrac{V}{kV}\right)}{(line\ voltage\ in\ V)\sqrt{3}}$$

For primary line current,

$$I = \frac{(200\ kVA)\left(1000\ \dfrac{V}{kV}\right)}{(480\ V)(1.732)} = 241\ A$$

For secondary line current,

$$I = \frac{(200\ kVA)\left(1000\ \dfrac{V}{kVA}\right)}{(240\ V)(1.732)} = 481\ A$$

For single-phase transformers,

$$I = \frac{(transformer\ rating\ in\ kVA)\left(1000\ \dfrac{V}{kV}\right)}{line\ voltage\ in\ V}$$

21. **C** If the temperature goes beyond the rated range for a heat pump's refrigerant, the system will not work. Heat pumps work on the same cycle as air conditioners, but the inside and the outside elements are reversed. Heat pumps do deliver more heat energy than the energy required to run them, which is precisely why heat pumps are used, because of their efficiency. Rather than creating heat, heat pumps move heat from one point to another. Particularly in large buildings or complexes, several heat pumps will be used in conjunction with the same heat sink.

22. **A** One ton of air conditioning equals 12,000 BTU per hour. Therefore,

$$\frac{120,000\ \dfrac{BTU}{hr}}{12,000\ \dfrac{BTU}{hr}{ton}} = 10\ tons$$

23. **C**   When the volume of sound is doubled, an increase of only 3 dB occurs. Therefore,

$$60 \text{ dB} + 3 \text{ dB} = 63 \text{ dB}$$

24. **B**   Metal halide and Freon are not fire extinguishing agents. Metal halide is a type of HID lamp, and Freon is a refrigerant used in air conditioning systems. Both carbon dioxide and Halon are fire extinguishing agents used to smother flames without liquids that would damage the contents of a building.

25. **A**   A leaching field allows liquid sewage not containing solid waste to slowly seep into the ground and dissipate. Gray water from plumbing other than toilets and urinals is usually recycled by filtering and sedimentation; it does not typically discharge into the leaching field. A septic tank is used to store solid waste until it is emptied, but a leaching field does not store anything. Septic tanks and leaching fields are often used in rural areas where a public sewage system is unavailable. They are not used to store storm water runoff. They need careful design and maintenance to operate properly.

26. **B**   Because of the requirements of thermal mass, insulation, shading devices, etc., passive solar designs have greater initial costs in building and installing. Their benefit comes from lower operating costs for heating, cooling, and lighting, not from lower construction costs. They still usually rely on backup mechanical and electrical systems to adequately control the building during extreme weather conditions such as stormy, sunless days. Passive solar design allows the heat and light radiation of the sun into the building during cold winter months and keeps it out during hot summer months. To store the insolated heat passively, thermal mass or phase change materials are used to store and slowly radiate the heat without large temperature swings.

27. **D**   A trap can be removed when the drain is clogged, but it does not usually have a cleanout and is not used for that purpose. It can catch grease, but the grease must be dissolved or removed so as not to clog the trap itself. Traps may catch small items before they wash down the drain, but that is not their purpose. The primary function of a trap is to prevent methane sewer gas, caused by decomposition of sewage, from entering the building.

28. **C**   The steam heat system already has pipes that can be used for the heat sink if they are in good condition or can be replaced with new pipes of about the same size. With a heat pump system, each unit can be billed separately, based on that unit's electrical usage. All the other systems are forced air systems requiring major modifications to accommodate the required ductwork. A multizone system would require a separate branch duct for each unit. A double duct system provides the required flexibility but needs two complete sets of ductwork for each unit, an expensive and obtrusive solution. A VAV system requires the least ducting but does not have the flexibility necessary to allow different units to be heated and cooled effectively or comfortably.

29. **C**   A catch basin collects surface runoff from a swale in the ground and directs it into a storm drain. It is used outside the building, in the parking and pavement areas, or on the site itself, not under the plumbing fixtures in the building. It does not function as a trap, only as a collector, and does not hold any runoff or overflow.

30. **B**   To calculate the absorptivity of a space, calculate the surface area (not the volume) and multiply that total by the coefficient of absorption of the surface material.

Therefore,

$$\begin{aligned} &[(2)(15 \text{ ft})(30 \text{ ft}) + (2)(15 \text{ ft})(60 \text{ ft}) \\ &+ (2)(30 \text{ ft})(60 \text{ ft})](0.04) \\ &= 252 \text{ sabins} \end{aligned}$$

31. **D**   The correct answer is 20 A. The formula for electrical current is $I = V/R$. Therefore,

$$I = \frac{120 \text{ V}}{6 \, \Omega} = 20.0 \text{ A}$$

32. **B**   EMT (electrical metallic tubing), also known as thinwall, is the thinnest of the metal conduits. It is galvanized and not acceptable for embedment into concrete. IMC (intermediate metallic conduit) is a steel conduit and is acceptable as rigid conduit. Flexible metal conduit (flex) comes both with and without a flexible waterproof jacket and may be used everywhere except underground. Rigid conduit has the same thickness as schedule-40 plumbing pipe and is the safest to use.

33. **C**   Wet standpipes are provided for both the occupants of the building and the fire department to connect hoses for additional flow and pressure in fighting fires. Every point of every floor must be within 30 feet

of the end of a 100-foot hose connected to the wet standpipe; therefore, the maximum distance to any point is 130 feet.

34. **A** High pressure sodium (HPS) lamps are the highest rated in efficiency and lifetime, developing approximately 110 lumens per watt with a 24,000-hour life expectancy. Unfortunately, they produce a light with poor color rendition. Metal halide is another high intensity discharge (HID) lamp which is very efficient, but it produces only about 80 lumens per watt with a lifetime of approximately 10,000 hours. Mercury vapor was the first HID lamp produced and has very poor color rendition while providing only 50 lumens per watt with a 24,000 hour lifetime. Ultralume fluorescents are not HID lamps but are slightly more efficient than mercury vapor, producing 60–80 lumens per watt with a lifetime range of 10,000 hours.

35. **B** Glare in a lighting system always refers to an extreme contrast in brightness between light sources and other surfaces. Neither very high illumination from the lighting nor reflections cause glare.

36. **D** Low voltage incandescent lamps operate at either 12 volts or 24 volts. This allows smaller filaments (such as tungsten-halogen housed in quartz envelopes) to withstand higher operating temperatures, producing more light with better color and slightly extending the lamp life. The major advantage, however, to the low-voltage lamps is that the smaller filament results in a much better focus of the beam for higher intensity and aim of the illumination for dramatic effects.

37. **B** Typical three-phase systems are 120/208 V and 277/408 V. The lower voltage is the line-to-neutral (wye) value and the higher voltage is the line-to-line (endpoint) value. The wye connection is symmetrical, so the voltage from each of the three-phase wires to the neutral is the same. That voltage is calculated by dividing the line-to-line voltage by the square root of 3 (1.73). Since the voltage between the wye and endpoint is known, multiply 120 volts by 1.73 to yield the line-to-line voltage of 208 volts.

38. **C** Rainfall and the resulting surface runoff is directed separately from sanitary waste because it is basically clean. It does not need treatment in a sewage treatment plant like sanitary sewage. If the two systems were combined, the resulting system would be overloaded by the high volume generated from storm water, and raw sewage would be forced to bypass the treatment plant and empty without proper treatment.

39. **C** With parallel resistances, the net effective resistance of the circuit is calculated by the following formula.

$$\frac{1}{R_{\text{total}}} = \frac{1}{R_1} + \frac{1}{R_2} + \frac{1}{R_3} + \ldots + \frac{1}{R_n}$$

Therefore,

$$R_{\text{total}} = \left(\frac{1}{4\,\Omega} + \frac{1}{8\,\Omega} + \frac{1}{8\,\Omega}\right)^{-1}$$
$$= 2.0\,\Omega$$

40. **A** The U-value is the reciprocal of the R-value, the sum of the resistances. Therefore,

$$\frac{1}{25.3\,\dfrac{\text{hr-ft}^2\text{-}°\text{F}}{\text{BTU}}} = 0.04\text{ BTU/hr-ft}^2\text{-}°\text{F}$$

41. **D** All of the components listed are integral parts of the refrigeration cycle. The refrigerant Freon is a special liquid (which is actually a gas) that circulates in a closed loop. A condenser increases the pressure and condenses the Freon before it circulates through an expansion valve. The expansion valve allows the liquid to evaporate through the evaporator coil, which absorbs the latent heat of the building. The Freon then circulates through the compressor, which increases the pressure of the Freon. The condenser coil then transfers the heat through an evaporative chiller, also called a cooling tower.

42. **B** To solve the problem, calculate the footcandle level using the inverse square law (since the light is perpendicular to the floor). Then multiply the footcandle level by the reflectance to arrive at the brightness on the floor in footlamberts. Since $E = I/d^2$,

$$E = \frac{4000\text{ candelas}}{(11\text{ ft})(11\text{ ft})} = 33.06\text{ footcandles}$$

$$(33.06\text{ footcandles})(0.60) = 19.8\text{ footlamberts}$$

43. **A** The best shape for a duct is one that has the least perimeter area to cause friction loss, pressure loss, and noise. Therefore, the most efficient shape would be a round duct, since it has the smallest perimeter area for the same cross-sectional area and capacity. The next best shape is a square duct, since it is closest in shape to a circle. Rectangular ducts become less efficient and cause greater friction loss as they become more rectangular, having more perimeter area

for the same capacity. The differing shapes are not equal in performance because of the differing perimeter areas.

44. C To solve this problem, it is important to know that one psi of water pressure can lift a column of water 2.3 feet high. For example, 10 psi can lift water 23 feet. If the water is to be lifted 96 feet [(8 stories)(12 feet)], dividing 96 feet by 2.3 feet per psi results in approximately 42 psi required for the lift. Since the hose bibb requires 30 psi of pressure to operate and 10 psi is lost due to friction, those two figures must be added to the 42 psi. Therefore,

$$42 \text{ psi [lift]} + 30 \text{ psi [fixture]} + 10 \text{ psi [friction loss]}$$
$$= 82 \text{ psi}$$

45. C Use the following equation to calculate cooling loads.

$$q_c = UA\Delta T$$

Substitute CLTD for ΔT. Cooling load temperature differential (CLTD) is also known as equivalent temperature difference (ETD). These values adjust for conduction, time lag, and radiation. Absorptivity and transmissivity are considered in the U-value. Convection is not relevant to the equation.

46. D In a fluid medium such as air or water, the thermal transfer process is called convection. Transmissivity is the measure of how easily radiation can transmit through a solid material. Radiation is the process of heat transfer between two solid objects separated from one another. Conduction is the heat transfer process between two objects in direct contact with one another.

47. A The heat pump system can use individual heat pumps that can be metered unit by unit. Although a fan coil system can have individual units, the supply of conditioned air is furnished from a central plant to each coil, making it difficult to individually meter usage. A multizone system uses different mixing boxes for each zone, but the airflow is separated at the HVAC source and there is only one plant for all the zones.

48. D Ground fault (circuit) interrupters (GFI or GFCI) are electrical shut-off devices required for any circuits serving wet locations such as bathrooms, kitchens, garages, and exteriors. They are also required on large high-voltage circuits such as 277/480-V 1000-A circuits. Even if everything is switched off, ground fault interrupters can detect a short circuit and/or continual current loss to ground and disconnect or break the circuit to provide instantaneous protection.

49. C Three-phase induction motors are typically larger motors that vary little in revolutions per minute, unless overloaded. Single-phase a-c motors come in many shapes and sizes, typically less than 3/4 horsepower. A d-c motor is used for small-scale applications, and for elevators, where smooth and even acceleration from a dead stop to high speed is important. Universal motors run on either a-c or d-c current and are variable in speed, so they are usually used in small appliances and tools.

50. B All light striking a surface is either transmitted, reflected, or absorbed. If the light but not the image is transmitted through the material, the material is translucent (such as frosted glass). If light is bounced off the material, the material is reflective, even though the image is transmitted through it (such as in ordinary mirror glass). If no light or image is transmitted through a material, the material is opaque. If both the light and the image are transmitted through the material, the material is transparent.

Materials and Methods Division

Sample Examination

1. Where is the use of marble most applicable?

   A. where aesthetics and economy are important
   — B. where extreme temperature changes may be encountered
   C. as a countertop material in a commercial kitchen
   D. in areas needing to be durable but requiring minimum maintenance

2. If an interior door were required to be 1½-hour rated with an Underwriters Laboratories B label, what would be required?

   A. a solid core with no glazed openings
   B. an automatic closing device
   — C. both of the above
   D. neither of the above

3. What are lightweight concrete roofing tiles usually attached with?

   A. elastic cement or mastic
   B. annular nails
   C. aluminum nails
   — D. steel nails

4. Why is the deterioration of metal due to galvanic reaction a problem?

   — A. Climatic moisture control is difficult to achieve.
   B. Corrosion-preventive alloys weaken metal.
   C. It is difficult to apply protective coatings to all metal parts.
   D. Most commonly used metals have high galvanic reaction.

5. Which of the following statements regarding concrete placement is generally incorrect?

   — A. Large quantities should be poured at one time so it can be distributed uniformly.
   B. For slabs, concrete placement should start at the far end so each successive batch will be poured against previously placed batches.
   C. Concrete that strikes against forms and rebars will cause separation and honeycombing.
   D. Walls should be poured starting at either end and working toward the middle.

6. Which of the following mixes of ingredients is appropriate for mortar used for gypsum partition blocks?

   A. one part masonry cement, three parts sand
   B. one part portland cement, one part lime putty, six parts sand
   — C. one part neat gypsum plaster, three parts sand
   D. one part portland cement, ¼ part lime putty, four parts sand

7. When should open-web steel joists be avoided?

   — A. when building loads are unevenly distributed
   B. when fire-resistive ratings are required
   C. when long spans are required
   D. when weather conditions would delay erection

8. What is the primary use of a moisture barrier?

   A. to moisture-proof a building
   B. to lower the relative humidity of a building
   C. to prevent heat loss from a building
   — D. to prevent condensation within a building

9. Where are thermal expansion joints of a building normally found?

    A. in sidewalks and driveways around a building

    B. where a new addition is attached to an existing building

    C. where two dissimilar materials are adjacent to each other

    D. all of the above

10. The Uniform Building Code requires firestopping in all concealed draft openings. Which of the following areas do not require firestopping?

    A. in spaces between duct penetrations and wood framing

    B. in exterior stud walls at floor and ceiling levels

    C. around the top and all sides of pocket door frames

    D. in all interior stud walls at the midpoint of the wall

11. Which paint finish is the best choice to reduce flame spread?

    A. vinyl-based

    B. rubber-based

    C. synthetic-resin

    D. oil-based

12. In which situation is light-gage steel framing preferable to wood stud framing?

    A. where a higher degree of fire resistance is wanted

    B. where neither high humidity nor great temperature differentials are encountered

    C. when cost is a prime factor

    D. when speed of erection is a prime factor

13. The area of glass used in a window is limited by its thickness and the wind load upon it. The Uniform Building Code allows the area to be increased for certain types of glass. Which type allows the greatest increase?

    A. wired glass

    B. heat-tempered glass

    C. laminated safety glass

    D. heat-strengthened glass

14. What does it mean for a building material to be incombustible?

    A. It will not readily support flames.

    B. It will not burn.

    C. It is not made of paper or wood.

    D. It has a minimum one-hour fire rating.

15. Mastics are used to seal joints against air, dust, and sound. Which of the following is not true of mastics?

    A. They are suitable for application by hand, gun, or trowel.

    B. They are plastic or flexible to permit movement between surfaces.

    C. They bond rapidly and remain durable in all weather.

    D. They are free from blisters, cracks, and runs under normal temperatures.

16. The conventional wall system for building is wood framing with 2 × 4 studs at 16 inches on center. What is the reason for this?

    A. Years of use have made this system the standard.

    B. This system easily accommodates precut wall panels and components.

    C. It would be too costly for manufacturers to modify their production methods and machinery.

    D. The size and spacing of this system is optimum for its efficient use.

17. With regard to glulam timber, which is true?

    A. Straight lengths can span up to 60 feet.

    B. The longest pieces of lumber commonly available are used for the laminations.

    C. Architectural grade has the finest appearance.

    D. Laminations are at least 1 1/2 inches thick.

18. As the architect of a 50-story office building, you must select the passenger elevators. Which of the following need not be considered?

    A. the height of the building

    B. the number of elevators assigned for emergency evacuation

    C. the building occupancy (one firm or several)

    D. the dimensions and weight of rooftop mechanical equipment

19. If timber piles are located below the permanent water table level, which of the following is true?

 — A. They should be pressure-treated with a bituminous compound.
   B. They should not be used under these circumstances.
   C. No more than half the pile should be in damp earth.
   (D.) Deterioration will not be a problem.

20. What are the standard dimensions of metal casement windows based on?

   A. traditional English measurements
   B. standard metric measurements
   C. standard 4-inch modules
 — D. standard brick masonry modules

21. When selecting and applying insulation, it is very important to know its U-value. Which of the following is not true of U-value?

 — A. It is expressed in BTU per hour.
   B. It depends on the thermal resistance of a building element.
   C. A higher U-value allows greater heat loss.
   D. It represents the amount of heat flow through a building element.

22. Where is gypsum board used in drywall construction?

   A. where areas may be subject to rough use
   B. where layers are bonded with adhesive for lamination
 — C. where a fire-resistant surface equivalent to plaster is required
   D. as a substitute for conventional interior plaster

23. What is a nonbearing wall as classified by the Uniform Building Code?

 — A. It is a wall that supports only its own weight.
   B. It is a wall without a footing.
   C. It is a wall with openings of more than half of its area.
   D. It is an interior wall.

24. Where is Type IV, low heat, portland cement used in concrete?

   A. for placement in very cold weather
   B. for general construction use
 — C. for large concrete pours
   D. in areas of high alkaline content

25. Which of the following fiber types would be best for the carpeting in a restaurant?

   A. acetate
 — B. nylon
   C. acrylic
   D. wool

26. The overall purpose of the Uniform Building Code is to protect the health, safety, and welfare of the public. To achieve this goal, upon what does the Uniform Building Code primarily focus?

   A. on problems caused by unregulated location, use, and occupancy
 — B. on dangers from fire or the lack of adequate fire resistance
   C. on dangers from inadequate structural design
   D. on problems caused by poor quality materials and/or workmanship

27. Where in construction are the terms *bedding*, *buttering*, *soap*, and *parging* used?

 — A. in concrete
   B. in masonry
   C. in plastering
   D. in veneering

28. Which statement about "softwood" and "hardwood" is not true?

   A. Most hardwoods are much harder than most softwoods.
   B. They are botanical terms that are not necessarily related to the wood's actual hardness.
   C. Balsa wood is one of the softest woods, yet it is actually a hardwood.
 — D. Softwood comes from broadleaf trees, whereas hardwood comes from conifers.

29. What is the difference between a joist and a rafter?

   A. A joist is a horizontal member and a rafter is a sloping one.
   B. A joist supporting a roof is a rafter, therefore the terms are interchangeable.
   C. A rafter is usually 2 inches thick, whereas a joist may be thicker.
 — D. A joist supports a ceiling while a rafter supports a roof.

30. Which statement about cement is most correct?

    A. It was invented by the ancient Roman builders.

    — B. It comprises the largest portion of a concrete mix.

    C. It unites nonadhesive materials.

    D. It is chemically inert in a concrete mix.

31. What are the reasons for using aggregates in a concrete mix?

    I. to alter appearances such as color or texture

    II. to increase or reduce the mix density

    III. to achieve better resistance to abrasion and weathering

    IV. to reduce material costs

    V. to counteract the binder's drying shrinkage or setting expansion

    A. I, II, and III

    B. II, III, and IV

    C. I, II, III, and V

    — D. I, II, III, IV, and V

32. Which of the following statements regarding the water-cement ratio of concrete is not true?

    — A. The strength of concrete increases as the water-cement ratio increases.

    B. The strength of concrete is the same for a given water-cement ratio regardless of the amount of aggregate embedded.

    C. A low water-cement ratio reduces shrinkage and increases durability.

    D. The water-cement ratio is usually expressed as a ratio of weight, not volume, of the cement used.

33. Which of the following mortar joints are recommended for the maximum weather protection of masonry?

    I. squeezed joint

    II. raked joint

    III. V joint

    IV. concave joint

    V. struck joint

    A. I and II

    B. I, II, and III

    — C. III and IV

    D. all of the above

34. Which of the following statements concerning the proper installation of built-up roofing is not true?

    — A. Apply felts shingle fashion, starting at the higher part of the roof.

    B. Mop solid under all felts.

    C. Lay felts with side laps greater than end laps.

    D. Broom or press felts into the bitumen when it is hot.

35. A test cylinder is taken from a concrete foundation pour. Immediately after it is taken, the cylinder is placed in direct sunlight and high ambient temperature for several hours. Will the test results be valid according to ASTM standards?

    A. They will be valid only if the cylinder is refrigerated within 8 hours of being taken.

    B. They will be valid only if the cylinder is tested within 48 hours of being taken.

    C. They will be invalid unless the cylinder is cured normally for 7 days after being taken.

    — D. They will be unconditionally invalid.

36. What is the primary reason a preservative treatment is applied to an exterior wood deck?

    A. to improve the architectural appearance

    — B. to resist decay due to moisture

    C. to reduce flammability in case of fire

    D. to prevent galvanic reaction with the metal fasteners

37. Which of the following materials is considered thermosetting plastic?

    I. alkyds

    II. polyester

    III. urea-formaldehyde

    IV. fluorocarbon

    V. polycarbonate

    A. I, II, and III

    B. I, II, and V

    C. II, IV, and V

    — D. all of the above

38. The terms *pedestal*, *mandrel*, and *jetting* are used in what method of concrete construction?

    — A. cast-in-place spread foundations

    B. drilled pier foundations

    C. tilt-up concrete construction

    D. piling construction

39. What is the proper method for protecting an insulated wood stud wall from moisture vapor in a building located in a cold climate?

  A. Provide a vapor barrier on the inside surface to prevent moist, heated interior air from migrating inside the wall.
  B. Provide a vapor barrier on the outside surface to prevent moist, cold exterior air from migrating inside the wall.
  C. Provide a vapor barrier on both the inside and outside surfaces to prevent moisture from migrating inside the wall from either side.
  D. Provide wood studs with a water preservative treatment to resist decay from any moisture migrating inside the wall.

40. Which is the correct statement regarding the noise reduction coefficient (NRC) rating of a material?

  A. Noise reduction is measured based on the amount of sound energy reflected by a material.
  B. Materials with NRC ratings of 0.50 are considered reflective.
  C. NRC ratings are usually given in increments of 0.05.
  D. A 0.10 difference in NRC can be detected by the human ear.

41. What would be the most likely reason for a roof deck to be constructed with gypsum concrete?

  A. The forms are inexpensive and can be reused indefinitely.
  B. The roof deck can be poured without the expense of steel reinforcing.
  C. The roof deck is flat and nonstructural.
  D. The roof deck needs increased fire resistance.

42. A building has been designed using a wood shingle roof with a 3:12 pitch. To save costs, the contractor has proposed switching to composition shingles. What other change must be made to accommodate this substitution?

  A. The sheathing would have to be made solid.
  B. The roof slope would have to be increased to at least 4:12.
  C. The flashing would have to be galvanized or aluminum.
  D. The roofing nails would have to be corrosion-resistant.

43. What would be the reason to use steel roof decking on a project?

  A. It can be connected easily with self-tapping screws.
  B. It can be installed quickly, efficiently, and economically.
  C. The roof deck does not require a shear diaphragm.
  D. It is highly durable and, even when unfinished, outlasts the life of the building.

44. For a beach house close to the ocean, what is the best choice of pattern for redwood siding to be applied (without regard to expense)?

  A. vertical board-and-batten
  B. vertical butt
  C. horizontal tongue-and-groove
  D. horizontal ship-lap

45. Which statement regarding the fire resistance of materials is correct?

  A. The particular use of a material determines its fire rating.
  B. Materials used in residences require a Class III flame spread.
  C. Building codes limit the allowable smoke density rating of materials to 250.
  D. Openings in a fire-rated wall must have the same rating as the wall construction itself.

46. Which of the following materials are incompatible with each other?

  A. aluminum and zinc
  B. steep asphalt and coal tar
  C. gypsum cement and Keene's cement
  D. steel and bronze

47. Which is the correct statement regarding the use of wood truss joists versus solid wood joists for floor construction?

  A. Material costs of truss joists are less expensive.
  B. Installation is easier with truss joists.
  C. Truss joints can be partially cut into and still retain their strength, unlike solid wood joists.
  D. Solid wood joists have less shrinkage than truss joists.

48. What is the best and most practical method to make an underfloor crawl space of a wood-frame building as dry as possible?

    A. Install a moisture vapor barrier between the subfloor and the finish floor.

    B. Coat the underfloor substructural members with two coats of exterior enamel paint.

    C. Install a tight and continuous moisture barrier on the ground.

    — D. Install underfloor foundation venting at the rate of 1 square foot per 50 linear feet of exterior wall.

49. What is the proper sequence for laying out the foundations to be excavated and constructed for a rectangular building?

    I. Square the building corners.

    II. Determine excavation limits with chalk lines.

    III. Drop a plumb line where building lines cross.

    IV. Erect batter boards.

    V. Attach lines to batter boards to denote building lines.

    A. I, IV, V, III, II

    — B. IV, I, III, V, II

    C. I, II, III, IV, V

    D. II, I, III, V, IV

50. Which of the following statements concerning the waterproofing of a concrete retaining wall is incorrect?

    A. The waterproof membrane is placed on the outside of the wall to prevent moisture from entering the interior.

    B. The subsurface foundation drain is located at the very bottom of the footing of the retaining wall.

    C. Gravel backfill should be used even if a waterproof membrane is placed against the exterior side of the retaining wall.

    — D. Water-retardant admixtures in the concrete will provide protection and eliminate the need for other waterproofing.

Examination Answers with Explanations

1. **D** Marble is highly decorative, durable, and distinctive, and it requires little maintenance. Although marble is aesthetically very pleasing, it is not able to withstand extremely high temperatures, it is easily stained by high concentrations of chemicals and acids, and it is relatively expensive to buy and install.

2. **D** An Underwriters Laboratories B label on a door designates that it is 1 1/2-hour rated and is usually used in exit stairways. The entire door assembly, including the door, frame, hardware, etc., must comply with this fire rating. The door must be equipped with a self-closing mechanism that closes and latches the door after it is opened. Automatic closing devices are used in a fire assembly when a door will normally be open but must close automatically when a sensor determines a temperature increase due to fire. This is typical for a 3-hour rated assembly. Class B assemblies are permitted to have glazed openings not exceeding 100 square inches. Three-hour Class A assemblies may not have any glazed openings. Neither statement refers to a Class B, 1 1/2-hour rated door assembly.

3. **C** Elastic cement is used to seal joints between roofing tiles but is not strong enough for attachment, which requires nailing. In selecting roofing nails, the most important consideration is that they are made of noncorrosive material, such as aluminum. Steel nails will rust, discolor, and fail due to corrosion. Annular nails are very strong but unnecessary as this is not of prime importance for this application.

4. **A** When dissimilar metals come in contact with moisture, galvanic reaction occurs, resulting in the corrosion of one or both metals. This reaction can be prevented by using compatible metals or by isolating one metal from another. Alloys and protective coatings prevent atmospheric deterioration but not galvanic corrosion. Moisture in the atmosphere is impossible to control, and creates galvanic activity no matter what. The drier the air, the slower the galvanic action, but eventually deterioration occurs.

5. **A** Concrete should be placed as close as possible to its final position. It should not be poured in large quantities and then redistributed over long distances because the mortar flows out more easily than the aggregate causing segregation. There is also the potential for weak bonding between layers. Separation will also occur if the concrete is poured from too great a height or strikes the forms or rebar, allowing the aggregates to settle at the bottom. In walls, concrete should be placed at the ends or perimeter to prevent water from collecting at the edges. For slabs, concrete should be placed into the face of previously placed concrete to avoid separation during working and leveling.

6. **C** Gypsum partition blocks are used as a plaster base for interior partitions needing light weight, fire resistance, and sound isolation. The mortar is job-mixed with sand and neat plaster. The other mortar mixtures are used with concrete or brick masonry.

7. **A** Open-web steel joists are prefabricated lightweight trusses. Their disadvantage is that they are not capable of supporting heavy, concentrated loads or ones not evenly distributed. They can be fireproofed by various means and are available in long spans. A distinct advantage of open-web steel joists is that they can be erected in any type of weather rather easily.

8. **D** As the temperature rises, the amount of moisture in the air increases as vapor. Relative humidity is the quantified expression of the amount of water in the air. Moisture in a building comes from its occupants and its mechanical equipment. When the air becomes saturated and vapor condenses, the air temperature is called the dew point. A building interior is usually maintained above the dew point, but some of the exterior envelope surfaces are not. This will create condensation on inside surfaces of walls, windows, etc. Porous construction is susceptible to moisture vapor infiltration and condensation. A vapor barrier can prevent this from happening. Usually made of plastic or metal foil, the barrier is installed on the warm side of the construction to be above the dew point. Choice C is sometimes true, but it is not the main reason for using moisture barriers.

9. **D** Temperature changes affect all building materials and components. All of the conditions would require expansion joints. Expansion joints allow for differential movement to prevent cracks and breakage. In addition to providing flexibility, they are often used to weatherproof and soundproof a building.

10. **D** The purpose of firestopping is to slow the spread of fire in concealed spaces. This is achieved by limiting open spaces in walls to 10 feet maximum. Solid 2-inch-thick blocking, the same depth as wood

framing, is used. Fireblocking is only required in walls at floor and ceiling levels unless the wall height exceeds 10 feet. Stud walls are often framed with blocking at the midpoint, but this is not required.

11. **B** Rubber-based paints are usually used as flame-retardant paint finishes. They are difficult to ignite and are self-extinguishing. Most oil-based paints are highly flammable. Most synthetics burn slowly and are somewhat hard to ignite. No paint finish, by itself, can prevent a fire.

12. **A** Where incombustible construction is required or desired, light-gage steel framing is the best choice. Steel framing is also better than wood because it will not shrink, twist, or swell, and is impervious to termites, rot, and temperature. It is more expensive than wood framing but no faster to erect. Other advantages are its strength, rigidity, and efficiency in allowing the penetration of piping and conduits through the punched openings in the steel studs.

13. **B** The Uniform Building Code allows the highest adjustment factor for tempered glass. The other special glass types are all stronger than window or plate glass but are used for different situations. Wired glass is used for fire-rated windows and doors. Laminated glass is used where breakage or vandalism may occur. Heat-strengthened glass is used in spandrels of curtain-wall construction.

14. **B** The meaning of incombustible is that it is unable to ignite or support combustion when exposed to fire. Therefore, an incombustible material cannot burn.

15. **C** Most mastics possess all of the qualities except rapid bonding, which is more typical of adhesives. Though mastics and adhesives are related products, they are distinctly different. The basic difference is that mastics seal materials, whereas adhesives bond materials.

16. **A** Conventional wood framing is one of the most economical ways to build, and most finish materials are sized to fit this standard. Wood framing is the basis for most building codes and industry practices. It is easy to shape and fasten, easy to change, and easy to work with. Because of this, it has become more of a tradition than a necessity. Actual structural design would allow for greater spacing than 16 inches on center. If other standards were adopted, manufacturers would modify their production.

17. **A** Single glulam spans of 60 feet are common (with spans of 100 feet possible). They are used for arches or trusses. One of the advantages of glulams is that they use short lengths of end-joined lumber to form the desired length without loss of strength. Premium grade is the finest in appearance for exposed construction, followed by architectural and industrial grades. Laminations are normally less than 2 inches thick but may be as thin as ¾ inch, especially for curving members used in arches.

18. **B** Both passenger and freight elevators are selected based on their load factors, both occupants and equipment. The height affects the speed of the cars. The number of firms served affects rush-hour service requirements. Equipment to be transported affects the requirements for freight elevators. Elevators would not be considered for use in emergencies because the possibility of electrical or mechanical failure makes them unsafe for emergency situations.

19. **D** Timber piles kept continuously wet will remain permanent without treatment and deterioration will not be a problem. If they are partly above the water level, standing in both wet and dry conditions, they should be treated with a creosote preservative.

20. **D** The standard sizes of metal casement windows are based on brick masonry modules because they originally were designed to be used in brick wall construction.

21. **A** All of the statements are true except choice A, which is incomplete. The U-value is expressed in BTU per square foot, per hour, per °F of temperature difference between inside and outside air.

22. **B** Gypsum board and conventional interior plaster are similar in many ways, but they cannot be used interchangeably. Since the surface finish of gypsum board is softer, it cannot be used in areas of rough usage. Because of the combustible paper faces, gypsum board does not have the same fire resistance as plaster. It is used with adhesives in laminated construction.

23. **A** A nonbearing wall, as defined by the Uniform Building Code, is a wall that does not support any load other than its own weight. It may or may not have a footing and/or have openings, and it may be interior or exterior.

24. **C** Portland cement is produced in several different types, each with characteristics for a particular use. For cold weather, Type III, high early-strength, is used to generate heat to counteract low temperatures. For general use, Type I, standard, would be used. Type V,

sulfate-resisting, is able to protect against chemical attack from sulfates found in high alkaline areas. Type IV, low-heat, is appropriate for large concrete pours where slow setting, which avoids the high heat normally created that could lead to serious cracking in the concrete work, is desired.

25. **C** The performance of carpeting depends on a variety of factors, not on pile fiber alone. Durability, aesthetics, and ease of maintenance are major considerations. In restaurants where food is served, resistance to alkali, acid, and stains is of primary importance. Foods and beverages cause staining and are moisture-laden. Therefore, the rate of absorption in carpet is a prime factor in its stain resistance. Acrylics perform best for this.

26. **B** All of the problems listed are addressed by the Uniform Building Code with comprehensive and detailed regulations and restrictions. The primary focus, however, is on the protection of life and property from fire danger. Fire has historically posed the greatest danger to the public and has resulted in the greatest human and structural loss to society. Therefore, the Uniform Building Code focuses the majority of its standards and the most restrictive regulations on fire-resistive construction and the dangers from fire.

27. **B** All of the terms are used in masonry construction. *Bedding* is the horizontal layer of mortar in which masonry is laid. *Buttering* means spreading the mortar with a trowel on a masonry unit before placing it. A half-brick that is split lengthwise is called a *soap*. The process of applying a coat of cement mortar to the back of a wall is known as *parging*.

28. **D** Most hardwoods are indeed harder than most softwoods. They are botanical terms not related to actual wood hardness but to differences in cellular structure. Though strange, balsa wood is in fact a hardwood. The untrue statement is that broadleaf or deciduous trees yield softwood while conifers or evergreens yield hardwood. In fact, the opposite is true.

29. **A** A joist is a small horizontal beam that supports either a floor or a ceiling. A rafter is a small sloping beam that runs from the eaves to the ridge of a roof and defines the roof pitch. The main difference between them is that joists lie flat and rafters slope. A joist may support a floor, ceiling, and/or roof, but would not be called a rafter. A rafter would not support a floor or a ceiling, therefore the terms are not interchangeable. Both joists and rafters are usually two inches thick but both may be thicker.

30. **C** The ancient Romans invented concrete, not cement. The largest portion of a concrete mix is aggregate, not cement. Aggregate is the ingredient in concrete that is chemically inert, not cement. Cement is the ingredient in concrete that unites the other nonadhesive materials to create a hard, strong, monolithic building material.

31. **D** Aggregates are added to concrete mixes for all of the reasons stated. Special aggregates may also be used to add some special quality to a mixture, such as fire resistance, thermal insulation, or acoustical properties. Lightweight aggregates are used to reduce the actual dead weight of the concrete to lighten the loads on a structure. There are even heavyweight aggregates used to provide shielding from radioactivity.

32. **A** The inverse of choice A is true: as the water-cement ratio increases, the strength of concrete decreases because of the higher water content. Using a workable mix with the lowest water-cement ratio that allows the ingredients to be thoroughly compacted yields the densest and strongest concrete.

33. **C** For maximum weather protection, tooled joints are recommended for masonry. The squeezed joint is a rustic, non-tooled joint and does not give a clean, weathertight joint. The raked joint, though it gives a strong horizontal shadow, may leak at the bottom and is not recommended either, although it is a tooled joint. Tooling the mortar into a V joint or a concave joint produces a good weather joint and both are highly recommended. A struck joint is not recommended because rain can be channeled into the bottom of the joint and into the masonry. Therefore, the V joint and the concave joint are the recommended methods of tooling masonry for maximum weather protection from wind and rain.

34. **A** Roofing felts are applied in shingle fashion, but they should be started at the lowest part of the roof. This method allows each successively higher felt to overlap the previous, lower felt, to provide maximum protection from the weather.

35. **D** Concrete must be kept cool and moist to properly cure for testing and proper strength when used in construction. If the cylinder is exposed to direct sunlight and high temperatures, it will be heated and dried too rapidly for proper testing of its strength. Refrigerating it after it has been exposed in this manner will neither counteract the improper exposure nor validate the test results of the cylinder. Testing within

48 hours, likewise, will yield inaccurate results and invalidate the testing procedure. Curing it for 7 days, when the first test is normally taken, will still yield inaccurate test results, once the cylinder has been initially exposed in this manner. Any test results from a cylinder exposed to such conditions will be unconditionally invalid according to ASTM standards for such test procedures.

36. **B** Although a preservative treatment will result in an improved architectural appearance for a wood deck, this is not the primary reason for treating the wood. To reduce flammability and provide fire resistance, fire-retardant lumber with special factory-applied chemical treatments, not field-applied preservatives, is used. Galvanic reaction occurs only between dissimilar metals and does not occur with wood. The primary reason a preservative treatment is applied is to protect wood from decay due to exposure to moisture, either from rain or from direct contact with the ground.

37. **A** Plastics are produced synthetically and can be shaped and molded. If a material is thermoplastic, it can be softened by heating and, upon cooling, it will regain its original properties. Examples of thermoplastics include acrylics, cellulose acetate, fluorocarbon, nylon, polycarbonate, and polystyrene. Thermosetting refers to the process using heat to cure the plastic to an infusible form that cannot be remelted. Alkyds, polyester, and urea-formaldehyde are thermosetting plastics, along with epoxy, melamine, and polyurethane.

38. **D** Piling construction uses the technical terms mentioned. A *pedestal* is the bulge of concrete formed at the end of a pile. A *mandrel* is inserted into a hollow pile to reinforce the shell while it is driven into the ground. Once the pile is driven to the depth required, the mandrel is removed and concrete is poured into the shell. To create a hole that is later filled with concrete, high-powered water jets are used, known as *jetting*. When conventional pile-driving might disturb adjacent structures, jetting is used to minimize the effect.

39. **C** In a cold climate, moisture vapor may migrate inside a wall from both the outside ambient environment and the inside heated spaces. A vapor barrier on only the inside will not protect the wall from the moisture in the outside air. Likewise, a vapor barrier on only the outside will not protect the wall from the moisture produced by the heated air inside the building. A vapor barrier should be provided on both sides of the wall to properly protect the interior of the wall from damage and decay caused by moisture. Special care must be taken to use materials on the cold side of the wall that will prevent moisture from entering while allowing any vapor trapped inside to escape to the outside. Although preservative treatment of the wood studs will prevent decay, it will not protect insulation materials in the wall, which can be damaged by moisture vapor and thus lose their effectiveness.

40. **C** Noise reduction is measured by the amount of sound energy absorbed by a material rather than reflected by it. An NRC rating of 0.70 means that 70% of the sound energy hitting the material is absorbed, with the other 30% being reflected. Materials with an NRC rating of up to 0.25 are considered reflective. Absorptive materials typically are rated between 0.25 and 0.75, with highly absorptive materials in the 0.80 to 0.90 range. Therefore, an NRC rating of 0.50 would not be considered reflective. NRC ratings are usually stated in increments of 0.05. The unaided human ear generally cannot detect a difference of only 0.10 in the NRC rating of a material.

41. **D** Gypsum concrete roof decks are usually poured over in-place forms supported by steel purlins, so the forms are permanent and cannot be reused. The deck is reinforced with either welded or woven wire mesh reinforcement so that expense is not avoided. Gypsum concrete can be used on almost any roof shape, size, or pitch, not only flat roofs, and is considered a structural roof deck. Gypsum concrete is commonly used for noncombustible construction to provide increased fire resistance. It is a factory-mixed combination of gypsum and wood chips or mineral aggregate that is mixed with water on site. When poured 2 inches thick over permanent formboards, the deck qualifies as a 1-hour fire-resistant construction. It sets quickly and is relatively lightweight and fire resistive.

42. **A** Composition shingles and wood shingles are very similar and can usually be used interchangeably, as they are both applied in the same overlapping fashion. Composition shingles, however, must be applied over solid sheathing (usually plywood), whereas wood shingles can be nailed over spaced sheathing with a maximum of 4 inches of clear space. Either type of shingle can be used for roofs with a minimum pitch of at least 3:12, so the slope would not have to be changed. Both types of roofing use similar flashings, either galvanized sheet metal, aluminum, or copper, and they also use similar nails—usually corrosion-resistant aluminum or hot-dipped galvanized steel.

43. **B** Although steel roof decking can be installed with screws, it is usually attached with normal welding equipment to give it added strength as a diaphragm. It is, however, installed quickly, efficiently, and economically, which is the principal reason it is used on many commercial buildings. Roof decks normally require shear diaphragms, and steel decking with specific attachments is often used for that purpose. Steel decking usually comes with a prime coat of paint or a hot-dipped galvanized finish for initial protection from the elements. Once it is installed, the final finish or roofing is applied to provide the required protection. If it were not finished with a protective covering, it would be susceptible to corrosive forces that would rust and deteriorate the steel quickly.

44. **C** For a house located close to the ocean, redwood or cedar siding is an excellent choice to weather the highly corrosive environment of the salt air. Its weak point, though, is its attachment and nailing to the structural framing. Steel nails should not be used. Hot-dipped galvanized, stainless steel, or aluminum nails are recommended. (Over time, they too will have some deterioration that causes streaking and staining of the redwood from the tannin.) Additionally, threaded nails are advisable to prevent the nails from working loose. Vertical board-and-batten or butt sidings both have exposed nails, as does the horizontal shiplap. Horizontal tongue-and-groove siding uses blind nailing where the nails are concealed to protect them from exposure to the corrosion.

45. **A** The fire resistance of materials is measured and rated according to their use in the building. Materials are rated in a number of different ways, depending on whether they are used for structural support, for containment and separation, or for exposed finishes and details that would contribute to flame spread and smoke development. Although Class III is the least fire-resistive classification, most residences do not normally require any flame spread rating for their materials because they are usually non-rated structures. Typical building codes limit the amount of smoke density for materials to 450 (not 250) although the construction materials industry is well ahead of this standard. Openings in fire-rated walls are required to be fire rated, but the ratings can be slightly lower than the partition rating. For example, a 1-hour wall may have 20-minute, 45-minute, or 1-hour opening protection, depending on the wall, its location, and its usage.

46. **D** Aluminum and zinc are two dissimilar nonferrous metals that are compatible with one another. They can be used together without causing the galvanic reaction observed in other dissimilar metals. Although plain asphalt and coal tar are not compatible with each other, steep asphalt (a special formula) and coal tar are compatible. Both gypsum cement and Keene's cement, as well as plaster of paris, are used for interior applications and are also compatible. Steel and bronze, being dissimilar ferrous metals, are not compatible and should be protected from deterioration by placing an intermediate material where they come in contact.

47. **B** Wood truss joists are being used more and more in light frame construction today. Although they are pre-engineered and prefabricated in factories for efficient production, they are usually more expensive in material cost than solid sawn lumber. Their benefit comes from their lighter weight, greater strength, and ease of handling and installation. With predetermined cutouts in the webs of the trusses, the installation of plumbing and electrical lines is considerably easier as well. Both solid lumber and truss joists can be cut only in certain areas without considerably reducing their strength. Truss joists should be cut only where the knockouts are predrilled and never through the top or bottom chords or they will lose virtually all of their structural capacity. Solid wood joists have much more shrinkage, which is a chief disadvantage, causing nails to pull loose, floors to squeak, and wall and floor finishes to crack and separate. Truss joists are dry and dimensionally stable, which limits their shrinkage.

48. **C** Moisture from the ground is usually the worst problem encountered in underfloor crawl spaces. Moisture in the earth can rise 10 feet above the water table, evaporate into the crawl space, and condense into liquid. This condensation causes the deterioration of organic materials such as the wood structural members and leads to the condition known as *dry rot*. Installing a moisture vapor barrier at the flooring would be of little value in controlling this type of moisture from the ground and would only prevent it from entering the living spaces above. Painting the members would preserve them from deterioration, but its cost would not be practical and would not keep the crawl space dry. In any case, the best method is to prevent moisture from accumulating in the first place. Installing a tight and continuous moisture barrier, such as polyethylene film at least 4 mils thick, is the best and most practical method

to prevent ground evaporation from entering the crawl space. This method should be combined with adequate underfloor ventilation, but the building code requires 1½ square feet for each 25 linear feet, not 1 per 50 linear feet.

49. **A**   Starting with a building corner and using a transit, the lengths and directions of the four sides are laid out. Once the corners are staked, batter boards are erected from 4 to 8 feet outside the building lines and are then leveled. Strings are attached to the batter boards directly over the building lines to denote where they occur. Where these string lines cross, a plumb line is dropped to set the corners exactly. Finally, the excavation limits, depending on the footing sizes, are chalked on the ground to guide the excavator in digging the foundation trenches.

50. **D**   To properly waterproof a retaining wall, a suitable waterproof membrane should be placed on the outside of the wall. This prevents moisture from the adjacent retained earth from entering the wall and migrating through to the interior. In addition, continuous subsurface foundation drains are placed at the bottom of the footing all along the wall in order to prevent any subsurface moisture from accumulating behind the wall or under the footing. These drains should likewise be laid at the bottom of a bed of gravel or drain-rock backfill extending the height of the wall to within 12 inches of the surface. The gravel carries any ground-water away from the wall and down to the foundation drain, preventing any hydrostatic pressure from building up behind the wall. Water-retardant admixtures for concrete are not used to waterproof a concrete wall and will not eliminate the need for positive waterproofing methods.

Construction Documents and Services Division

Sample Examination

1. What are performance specifications concerned with?

    A. generic products
    B. final results
    C. methods of fabrication
    D. specific dimensions

2. What is the most important reason for using fast-track scheduling?

    A. to reduce the cost of professional services
    B. to shorten anticipated construction time
    C. to decrease the overall hard costs of construction
    D. to guarantee project costs prior to construction

3. Who is responsible for coordinating the location of HVAC ductwork with the location of the structural framing?

    A. the architect
    B. the mechanical engineer
    C. the structural engineer
    D. the contractor

4. Which of the following are contract documents in a Project Manual?

    A. Instructions to Bidders
    B. Geotechnical Investigation and Soils Report
    C. Supplementary Conditions
    D. Bid Bond

5. Which is true about a performance specification?

    A. It requires less work by the architect.
    B. It can be used for most building materials.
    C. It allows the contractor to be innovative.
    D. All of the above are true.

6. In a small residential project, which of the following is most likely to be described by a performance, design-build specification?

    A. waterproofing systems
    B. electrical systems
    C. truss framing
    D. roofing

7. What is the common or usual method to ensure that the final set of construction documents satisfy the client's program and design goals?

    A. Make a checklist of program requirements for the staff working on the project to use to continuously monitor their progress as they prepare the drawings.
    B. Have the client review a final check set for compliance with the program requirements and request that any corrections be noted.
    C. Have another architect who is unfamiliar with the project review the final set for compliance with the original program requirements.
    D. Hold regular progress meetings with the client and staff involved to compare the current status of the drawings with the original program requirements. At the conclusion of this phase, require that the client provide the architect with written approval to proceed to the next phase.

8. What does the abbreviation ASTM represent?

    A. American Standard Testing Method
    B. Association of Specialty Trade Manufacturers
    C. American Society for Testing and Materials
    D. American Specifications and Test Methods

9. Where in the Project Manual would a contractor look to find the requirements for testing an HVAC system?

    A. Part 1 of Section 15500 Heating, Ventilating, and Air Conditioning
    B. Part 3 of Section 15500 Heating, Ventilating, and Air Conditioning
    C. Division 1—General Requirements
    D. Part 3 of Section 15990 Testing, Adjusting, and Balancing

10. Which of the following would be preferable to use in specifying waterproofing for use behind a below-grade concrete retaining wall?

    A. base bid with approved alternate manufacturers
    B. base bid or equal
    C. performance standards
    D. base bid with no equal

11. If a specification is in conflict with a note on the drawings, which statement is correct?

    A. Details take precedence over notes.
    B. Details take precedence over drawings.
    C. Specifications take precedence over drawings.
    D. Drawing notes take precedence over specifications.

12. Sequencing and Scheduling; Delivery, Storage and Handling; and Maintenance are found in what part of a technical specification?

    A. Part 1
    B. Part 2
    C. Part 3
    D. any of the above

13. What are the three parts in a CSI format specification?

    I. General
    II. Scope
    III. Materials
    IV. Products
    V. Performance
    VI. Execution

    A. I, III, and V
    B. I, IV, and VI
    C. II, III, and V
    D. I, III, and VI

14. Which of the following statements about specifications is false?

    A. Narrowscope and broadscope sections cannot be used together.
    B. Proprietary specifications are the same as prescriptive specifications.
    C. Drawings show quantity and location; specifications show quality and execution.
    D. Specifications are not open to interpretation if they are base bid. ?

15. What is the likely result of specifying both the results and a method for achieving those results in a masonry specification?

    A. The specification will achieve the desired intent exactly.
    B. The specification may be impossible to achieve.
    C. The specification will raise the costs of compliance.
    D. The specification will allow the contractor latitude in achieving either the results or the method.

16. For a contractor, which of the following is least important for bidding purposes?

    A. the number of separate trades required on the project
    B. the number of times equipment is needed at the site
    C. the types of tools needed to build the project
    D. the time of commencement of the project

17. What is the usual sequence of architectural drawings?

    I. Floor Plans
    II. Exterior Elevations
    III. Building Sections
    IV. Reflected Ceiling Plans
    V. Interior Elevations

    A. I, II, III, IV, V
    B. I, IV, III, II, V
    C. I, III, II, V, IV
    D. I, IV, II, V, III

18. Where should the architect note the thickness and gage of a galvanized sheet metal gravel stop roof flashing?

    A. roof plan
    B. wall section through roof
    C. detail at edge of roof
    D. Specification Section 07600

19. What is a reliable method for the architect to use to furnish the owner with an Estimate of Probable Construction Cost once the Construction Documents are complete?

    A. cost per square foot for similar construction types
    B. cost per cubic foot for similar construction types
    C. quantity survey and labor and material take-off
    D. all of the above

20. What is the purpose of an expansion joint?

    A. to allow for a future addition to the building
    B. to allow for any anticipated movement in the building
    C. to allow for dissimilar materials to not be in direct contact
    D. to expand and provide a weathertight joint between materials

21. After the bid documents are issued, the owner requests additional work to be included in the contract for construction. What document should the architect issue?

    A. Construction Change Directive
    B. Change Order
    C. Addendum
    D. Modification

22. What does a Change Order change?

    I. the scope of project
    II. the time of completion
    III. the cost of project
    IV. the design of project
    V. any change in the work

    A. I and II
    B. II and III
    C. II, III, and IV
    D. V

23. The concrete subcontractor is preparing to pour concrete for a foundation when the architect notices that some reinforcing steel is omitted. What should the architect do?

    A. Stop the work and direct the placement of the reinforcement.
    B. Stop the work and notify the concrete subcontractor.
    C. Notify the owner and the contractor in writing.
    D. Stop the work and notify the building inspector.

24. If there is a dispute or claim between the owner and the contractor, how is it resolved according to AIA General Conditions?

    A. It is submitted for architect's decision as final.
    B. It is submitted for architect's decision, subject to arbitration.
    C. It is submitted to binding arbitration.
    D. It is submitted to a court of law.

25. Contract documents require certain tests and inspections. Who is usually responsible to pay for them?

    A. the owner
    B. the architect
    C. the contractor
    D. the subcontractor

26. How is safety handled on any construction project?

    A. Follow specific requirements found in the Project Manual.
    B. Have the owner employ a job safety inspector to monitor safety.
    C. Safety is handled in accordance with AIA General Conditions.
    D. Safety is solely the responsibility of the general contractor.

27. The supplier has sent the architect a sample of carpeting that was specified in the Project Manual, with a request that the architect review and approve it. What should be done?

    A. Return it without reviewing it.
    B. Review it to check if it conforms to the specifications.
    C. Review and approve it if it conforms to the specifications.
    D. Review it for conformance to the design intent only.

28. What does the term *Substantial Completion* indicate?

    A. The requirements of the contract documents have been met and the project is suitable for its intended occupancy by the owner.

    B. The project is complete and the contractor is owed the final payment.

    C. All punchlist items have been completed by the contractor.

    D. All of the above are correct.

29. To close out a project, what is the proper order for the following tasks?

    I. notification by contractor that project is ready for final inspection

    II. preparation of punchlist

    III. issuance of certificate of substantial completion

    IV. receipt of consent of surety

    V. preparation of certificate for final payment

    A. I, II, III, IV, V

    B. II, I, III, IV, V

    C. III, II, I, IV, V

    D. II, I, III, V, IV

30. According to AIA General Conditions, when does an architect need to respond to a contractor's claim for additional contract time caused by inclement weather?

    A. within 7 days

    B. within 10 days

    C. within 14 days

    D. within a reasonable period of time, depending on the nature of the claim

31. For how long after completion is the contractor usually obligated to correct defective work under the contract documents?

    A. for 1 year

    B. for 5 years

    C. for 10 years

    D. for the life of the building

32. When does the contractor submit a "Schedule of Values" to the architect?

    A. with the completed bid form

    B. after the bid but before the signing of the contract

    C. after the signing of the contract, before construction starts

    D. prior to the first application for payment

33. Which of the following statements is false?

    A. The contractor is responsible for property insurance for the project until it is completed.

    B. The contractor is responsible for liability insurance for the project until it is completed.

    C. The owner is responsible for property insurance for the project until it is completed.

    D. The owner is responsible for loss-of-use insurance for the project until it is completed.

34. A portion of the work has been covered without the architect observing it. Although not specifically requested in the contract documents, the architect wants the work uncovered so it can be checked. When it is uncovered, it is found to be in conformance with the contract documents. Who is responsible for the costs of uncovering and replacing the work?

    A. the architect

    B. the owner

    C. the contractor

    D. costs are shared equally by all three

35. According to AIA General Conditions, an application for a progress payment dated June 30 is submitted by the contractor to the architect on June 20. When must the architect either issue a certificate for payment or notify the contractor in writing that the certificate is being withheld?

    A. immediately upon receipt of the application

    B. by June 27, since that is within 7 days of receipt of application

    C. by June 30, since that is when the progress payment is due

    D. by July 7, since that is within 7 days of the due date of the progress payment

36. Regarding allowances in a contract sum, which statement is true?

    A. Allowances are for the cost of materials and installation.

    B. Allowances are not included in the contract sum.

    C. Allowances are for the cost of materials only.

    D. Allowances are for the cost of materials, handling, profit, and overhead.

37. Where are the General Conditions of the Contract for Construction normally placed?

  A. in the Agreement
  B. in the Drawings
  C. in the Specifications
  D. in the Project Manual

38. Who owns the copyright to the architect's construction documents once a project is built?

  A. the architect, since they are the architect's property
  B. the owner since he or she owns the project and paid for the architect's services
  C. the contractor, since the documents were used to build the completed project
  D. no one, as they are public record once a project is built

39. What is the purpose of a Performance Bond?

  A. to withhold money from a contractor's payment to ensure that work is completed and corrected
  B. to ensure that some third party will complete the project if the contractor does not
  C. to guarantee that a contractor will perform within the contract time limits
  D. to protect the owner against any mechanic's liens being filed

40. The architect is the agent of the owner. What does that mean?

  A. The architect has the authority to act on the owner's behalf.
  B. The architect is the intermediary principal of the contract between the owner and contractor.
  C. The architect is solely responsible to the owner.
  D. The architect assumes all the owner's normal responsibilities.

41. What is the appropriate scale for detail drawings of a threshold?

  A. $1/4$ inch equals 1 foot
  B. $3/4$ inch equals 1 foot
  C. 3 inches equals 1 foot
  D. full scale

42. During construction, the contractor notices that the dimensions of a spandrel detail drawing do not match those shown in the overall building section drawing. What should the contractor do?

  A. Follow the building section as it shows how the building works as a whole.
  B. Follow the detail drawing since it is at a larger scale.
  C. Notify the architect of the discrepancy and ask for clarification.
  D. Refer to specifications and obtain the exact dimensions from the manufacturer.

43. Which of the following situations would not normally need to be detailed in a set of construction drawings?

  A. roof-to-wall flashing
  B. window head
  C. grade beam connection to pier
  D. fireblocking of interior wall

44. In detailing an 8-foot-high concrete retaining wall, which is the correct statement?

  A. A waterproof membrane is placed on the unexposed face of the wall.
  B. A waterproof membrane is placed on the exposed face of the wall.
  C. Protection board can be omitted if drain rock is used.
  D. Perforated drain pipe can be omitted if drain rock is used.

45. Which of the following wall details meet the ICBO minimum requirements for a 1-hour rated wall assembly?

  A. 2×4 wood studs with $1/2$-inch fire-rated gypsum board on both sides
  B. 2×4 wood studs with $5/8$-inch fire-rated gypsum board on both sides
  C. $1 5/8$-inch metal studs with $1/2$-inch fire-rated gypsum board on both sides
  D. $1 5/8$-inch metal studs with $5/8$-inch fire-rated gypsum board on both sides

46. What would be the preferred method of applying ceramic tile to the concrete floor of a restaurant kitchen?

    A. waterproof epoxy cement
    B. thin-set grout
    C. cement mortar
    D. tile adhesive

47. Which lock would be the best for a door to a commercial office?

    A. a rim lock
    B. a unit lock
    C. a cylindrical lock
    D. a mortise lock

48. In designing and detailing a high-rise apartment building, which of the following statements is true?

    A. Sprinkler systems and refuge areas must be provided.
    B. Class I interior finishes must be provided throughout.
    C. The building must have at least three stairways.
    D. All of the above are true.

49. What areas of a privately owned high-rise office building built in 1994 are required to meet the minimum requirements for accessibility for the physically disabled?

    A. entrances, corridors, elevators, and restrooms
    B. entrances, corridors, and exitways
    C. any area used by the general public
    D. all areas of the building

50. An interior casework detail specifies kiln-dry, vertical-grain Douglas fir shelving. How much moisture content can the wood have?

    A. 0 percent
    B. 10 percent
    C. 15 percent
    D. 19 percent

Examination Answers with Explanations

1. **B** Performance specifications describe a desired result rather than how to achieve that result. For example, an HVAC system may be performance specified by indicating temperature limits, humidity ranges, air flow, distribution, etc., without calling out a specific product, system, or manufacturer. The details of how to achieve the desired results are left to the contractor to determine, as long as the completed system performs to the standards specified.

2. **B** Fast-track scheduling is the best means available to shorten the time between the start and finish of a construction project. Using fast-track methods, the architect prepares separate bid packages prior to final completion of construction documents, making it impossible to know final overall costs until construction is well underway. These separate bid packages increase the architect's services, thus increasing the costs and fees. Fast-track scheduling does not reduce construction costs, but it does reduce construction time, which can in turn reduce project financing costs and cost increases due to inflation over a longer period of time.

3. **A** The architect is the design professional responsible for all coordination of the various components of the related disciplines involved in the building design. It is the architect's job to verify that none of the components interfere with any other.

4. **C** Bid Bonds and Instructions to Bidders may be included in the Project Manual for bidding purposes, but they are not considered part of the contract for construction between the owner and contractor. The Geotechnical Investigation and Soils Report may or may not be included in the Project Manual. They are for information only. Supplementary Conditions are additions, deletions, revisions, and modifications to the General Conditions. As the General Conditions are contract documents for the contract for construction, Supplementary (and Special) Conditions are contract documents as well.

5. **C** Performance specifications are more difficult to research, write, and review so they require more, not less, work for the architect. Most building materials and requirements are so well established in the construction industry that there is no need for performance specifications. Building codes sometimes require that certain materials be precisely specified to determine their code compliance and will not allow a performance specification. Performance specifications do allow the contractor and the subcontractors to be innovative in the way they supply the materials to meet the performance specified, which often reduces costs and scheduling.

6. **B** To reduce initial costs in small residential projects, electrical and mechanical engineering consultants are often not used. In such cases it would be appropriate for the architect to specify electrical and mechanical systems, such as HVAC, by a performance specification to the subcontractor who would design the actual system up to codes and build it to that design and specification. Waterproofing and roofing (which is a type of waterproofing) are critical areas involving many systems and details working together and are best for the architect to design and detail, specifying exactly what will be required. Truss framing is usually designed and specified by the architect and/or structural engineer for proper coordination. Actual detailed engineering and/or details must be furnished as shop drawings by the truss manufacturer to comply with the design as specified, but this is not a performance or design-build procedure.

7. **D** A checklist is a good method to use, but staff are usually responsible for specialized tasks and cannot see that the overall design goals of the program are being met. Check sets are usually the architect's, not the client's, responsibility, and having the client review the final check set will be too late in the process to make corrections. Peer review, by another architect, is a good method for technical corrections, but is an unsatisfactory method for checking program and design compliance. Regular meetings with the client and the staff involved in programming, design, and production is the best way to facilitate communication and ensure compliance with the client's requirements. Obtaining written approval from the client before proceeding to the next phase in the project formalizes the agreement, preventing future misunderstandings.

8. **C** ASTM is the abbreviation for the American Society for Testing and Materials. The ASTM is a trade association that develops industry standards for testing various materials and products used in the construction industry. ASTM standards are frequently utilized in building code requirements and specification references.

9. **D** Typically, each section of the specifications will specify the proper testing procedures in Part 3–Execution, if it is appropriate. Because the testing, adjusting, and balancing of HVAC systems is critical to their effectiveness and efficiency, a separate Section 15990 is usually included to cover those procedures. Part 1 of Section 15500 deals with the general requirements and scope of work. Part 3 of Section 15500 specifies the method of execution for the work. Division 1—General Requirements outlines the general procedures for the contractor on the entire job, rather than on any one specific section.

10. **A** A base bid with approved alternate manufacturers is preferable to allow the contractor latitude in selecting products based on their cost and availability. A base bid with an "or equal" clause gives the contractor too much latitude in selecting a product that they feel is equal because the architect is not given the opportunity to review and approve or disapprove the product. Performance standards would not normally be used for a product as important as waterproofing. A base bid with no equal could raise the cost to the owner needlessly if other products are available at lower in-place costs. Furthermore, it could also disrupt the contractor's schedule if that product is not readily available, which would also raise the costs to the owner.

11. **C** Drawings do not usually take precedence over specifications, nor do notes or details take precedence. When conflicts such as this arise, specifications are much more detailed and informative and usually take precedence over drawings. In courts of law, this principle has usually been upheld. This order of precedence though, must be fully specified and/or noted in the contract documents by the architect to establish the priority of information in case of conflicts.

12. **A** Sequencing and Scheduling; Delivery, Storage, and Handling; and Maintenance are all found in Part 1 of a technical specification section. Part 1 deals with the general requirements of the particular trade or product covered by the specification. Part 2 deals with product requirements, while Part 3 deals with standards of execution.

13. **B** The three-part format developed by the Construction Specifications Institute (CSI) is as follows

   Part 1—General
   Part 2—Products
   Part 3—Execution

14. **A** Proprietary specifications are the same as prescriptive specifications. Drawings are intended to show the quantity and location of various materials, while specifications are intended to note the quality and the execution of materials and installation. If specifications are base-bid type, they are not open to interpretation by the contractor. In writing specifications, both narrowscope and broadscope sections can be used.

15. **B** In specifying a material, either the methods to achieve the results should be specified, or the resulting product, but not both. If both methods and results are specified, the specified product may not meet the requirements of the method specified, such as an ASTM standard. This would not achieve the desired intent and would create an impossible situation where the contractor could not comply with both requirements. Costs would not be affected if the specification were impossible to achieve, nor would the contractor have any latitude in complying with the specification.

16. **C** The number of separate trades required on a project is important to a contractor because it will have time and cost implications. The type and frequency of equipment and machinery used on the project site is also important because of costs and scheduling. Likewise, the date of a project's commencement has scheduling considerations for the contractor that may affect the costs. The least important issue is the types of tools because they are normally available and are not a significant part of the overall cost.

17. **C** The normal sequence of architectural drawings (as recommended by the American Institute of Architects *Handbook of Professional Practice*) is a Site Plan and Demolition Plan (if any), Floor Plans, Schedules, Building Sections, Exterior Elevations, Interior Elevations, Reflected Ceiling Plans, Exterior Details, and Interior Details. These architectural drawings are then followed by the consultant drawings, Structural, Mechanical, Plumbing, and Electrical.

18. **D** Normally, the thickness and gage of a material like galvanized sheet metal flashing should be noted only once in one document, Specification Section 07600–Flashing and Sheet Metal. The drawings may have details or sections indicating the location and dimensions of the gravel stop, but to avoid errors in case of conflicting information, they should avoid being redundant in specifying requirements and properties.

19. **C** At the stage where the Construction Documents, both drawings and specifications are completed, the only appropriate and reliable method to estimate construction costs is a detailed quantity survey with a labor and material take-off of all the work involved.

Cost per square foot or cubic foot estimates would be appropriate only at the schematic or design development stages, when details and specifications are still being changed and developed.

20. **B** The purpose of an expansion joint is to allow for movement of a building without causing rupture or cracking in the materials. All buildings will experience some movement, whether due to live or dead loads, differential settling, lateral forces, water absorption, temperature changes, or other causes.

21. **C** During the bidding process, any additions or deletions to the contract work should be addressed in an Addendum that is sent to every contractor who is bidding the project. A change to the actual construction contract would be made by a Modification. During the construction process itself, any changes are made by a Change Order, or if the exact cost of the change has not yet been determined, by a Construction Change Directive.

22. **B** A Change Order is a document that authorizes a change from the original contract documents in either the contract price, the contract time, or both. The scope of the project, the design of a project, or any other change may be handled by other documents if they do not involve changes in cost or time. Examples would be clarifications, interpretations, written orders, or field orders, all authorizing minor changes in the work that do not require changes to time or cost.

23. **C** Since the construction contract is between the owner and the contractor, the architect does not have the legal right to stop the work. Stopping the work may actually incur additional liability to the architect. The proper procedure would be to first notify the general contractor (not the subcontractor) to allow the general contractor to make the decision. Then the owner should be notified of the problem. If the foundation is poured without proper reinforcing, it could create a safety problem of which the building inspector should be aware. Definitely, both the owner and the contractor should be further notified in writing as soon as possible.

24. **B** There are usually claims and disputes on any construction project. AIA General Conditions specify that they should first be submitted to the architect for review and final decision. The architect's final decision, however, is subject to binding arbitration if the parties do not agree with the architect's decision. Litigation in a court of law is usually employed only when problems that are not covered by the contract between the owner and the contractor arise (such as damages to third parties).

25. **C** Certain tests and inspections by testing agencies and public authorities are normally required by the contract documents for a project. The provision for their scheduling and payment is the contractor's responsibility by the General Conditions, AIA Document A201. If the testing and inspection requirements were made after the bids were received or contract negotiations were concluded, the owner would bear the costs. In either case, the independent agencies performing these tests and inspections must be acceptable to the owner, as they are for the owner's benefit and protection. Sometimes, the general contractor may ask the subcontractors to figure these costs in their bids, but they are not contractually responsible for them. Upon notification by the contractor of when the tests and inspections take place, the responsibility of the architect is to observe them and then review the results for compliance with specifications. In some cases, the owner may prefer to contract directly with the testing lab. That is particularly true if the owner is a governmental entity or major corporation that builds on a continual basis and regularly contracts directly with a select group of testing labs.

26. **D** The general contractor is solely responsible for on-site job safety. The architect should not take responsibility for those provisions in the Drawings, Project Manual or in the field. Nor should the owner take on that responsibility by employing a job safety inspector. AIA General Conditions do not specify safety requirements either, other than to note that they are the contractor's sole responsibility.

27. **A** All submittals called for in the Project Manual should be first reviewed and approved by the general contractor. Then the submittals are transmitted to the architect for review and approval for conformance to the design intent only. If the submittal is received directly from a subcontractor or a supplier without the contractor reviewing and approving it, the architect should return the submittal without reviewing it. No review or approval should be done without the contractor's initial approval of the sample.

28. **A** The term *Substantial Completion* technically refers to the requirements of the contract documents being substantially met so that the project can be occupied for its intended purpose by the owner. This requires that all final inspections be done by public agencies before occupancy. Minor additional work may still be left to

finish or touch up, however, hence the need for a final punchlist of items needing correction. The final payment is not due until the job is fully completed and all contracted work on the project has ceased.

29. **B** The preparation of the punchlist is done first, before calling for final inspection. Once those items are completed, the contractor can call for final inspection by the building official. When the final inspection is passed, the project can be occupied, so the architect can issue the Certificate of Substantial Completion. The consent of any surety involved in the project must then be received before the architect can prepare and issue the certificate for final payment.

30. **B** AIA General Conditions, Document A201, requires that the architect respond within 10 days. The type or nature of the claim has no bearing on this requirement.

31. **A** The contract documents typically specify that the contractor will warranty the work of the project for 1 year from the date of substantial completion. Certain materials specified for the project, such as appliances or roofing, may carry longer warranties, however. This one-year warranty period is only for correction of defects in the work itself. This should not be confused with the general public or property liability of the contractor for any construction that may cause damage after the warranty period expires. Individual state laws regulate the time period in which a contractor may be held liable for so-called "latent" defects that often arise long after the project is completed.

32. **D** AIA General Conditions specify that the Schedule of Values should be submitted by the contractor to the architect before the first application for payment. The architect uses the Schedule of Values to assess the completion of various portions of work while certifying contractor's payments.

33. **A** AIA General Conditions specify that the owner, not the contractor, is responsible for property insurance for the project. The other statements regarding the owner's and contractor's responsibilities for insurances required for the project are all true. Loss-of-use insurance, however, is an option for the owner.

34. **B** If the work uncovered is in conformance with the contract documents, the owner is responsible for the costs of uncovering and replacing it. The architect is acting in the owner's best interests and does not incur any direct financial liability for such a condition. If the work is not in conformance, the contractor would be responsible for those costs, unless the condition was caused by the owner or the owner's separate contractor.

35. **B** Applications for progress payments are to be submitted at least 10 days before the date they are due. The architect must either issue the certificate for payment to the owner or notify in writing that it is being withheld within 7 days of receipt of the application. As the application was received June 20, 7 days would make June 27 the due date for the architect's action. Once the owner receives the architect's certification of payment, the owner makes the payment according to the actual schedule in the contract.

36. **C** Allowances are for the contractor's cost of materials only, less any trade discounts. Other costs such as installation, handling, profit, and overhead should be properly included in the contract sum and not in the allowances. The actual amount figured as an allowance, though, is included in the contract sum, and that sum is adjusted as necessary when the actual costs are documented by the contractor.

37. **D** The General Conditions of the Contract for Construction are part of the contract documents. Although they are usually referenced in the Agreement, the Drawings, and the Specifications, they are actually found in whole in the Project Manual itself.

38. **A** The construction documents, including drawings, specifications, and other documents prepared specifically for the project, are instruments of the architect's service. They are considered to be owned by the architect as intellectual property. The owner pays for the architect's services, not the product of those services. The contractor has no ownership, either, only a right to use the documents for the specific project being built under the contract. Even though the documents are submitted to public agencies for approval and become part of the public record, it is not considered publication per se in derogation of an architect's copyright.

39. **B** A Performance Bond may be required by the contract documents to ensure the contractor's performance in completing the project. A third party, known as a surety, issues the bond in favor of the owner. The cost is usually paid by the contractor but included in the contract sum to the owner. Withholding money from a contractor's payments is known as retainage. If the contractor fails to perform within the contract time limits, it is a breach of contract and is subject to remedies as specified in the contract. Labor and material payment bonds are used to protect the owner against any liens that are filed by payment of them should they occur.

40. **A** The principle of agency allows the architect to act on behalf of the owner with certain duties and responsibilities specified by their agreement. The architect is not a principal, intermediary or otherwise, to the contract between the owner and contractor. As a design professional licensed by each state, the architect cannot be solely responsible to the owner, but must safeguard the health, safety and welfare of the public at large. This public responsibility may occasionally override the architect's commitment to the owner. Acting as one's agent does not confer one's normal responsibilities on the agent, such as obeying laws, paying taxes, etc.

41. **C** Detail drawings are usually drawn at a scale where 3 inches equal 1 foot, or quarter scale. ¼-inch scale is normally used for plans, building sections, and elevations. ¾-inch scale is normally used for wall sections and other detailed sections. Full scale drawings are rarely used as they require too much space.

42. **C** In cases of conflict between smaller scale drawings such as building sections and larger scale detail drawings, the larger scale details normally take precedence. The proper procedure would be for the contractor to notify the architect of the discrepancy and request clarification. Discrepancies such as this may have extensive ramifications of which the architect must be aware. Referring to specifications and product literature at this stage may not satisfy the design intent of the architect. Such matters should be left for the architect to decide what is intended.

43. **D** Roof-to-wall flashing is extremely important and should normally be detailed to ensure watertightness. The same is true of detailing window heads to provide for proper watertight flashing and shim space to allow for movement. The connection of a grade beam to a pier is critical to the structural design and is usually thoroughly detailed in the structural drawings. Fire-blocking of an interior wall, however, is not usually detailed as it is a standard code requirement and typical construction with which all contractors are familiar. These types of typical details are not usually required.

44. **A** Waterproof membranes applied to the exposed face (usually interior) do not prevent moisture from penetrating the wall itself. A concrete retaining wall should be detailed with a waterproof membrane applied to the unexposed face (usually exterior) of the wall. This is done to prevent moisture from coming in contact with the wall and migrating through the wall.

Protection board is then installed to protect the membrane from the drain rock that is backfilled behind the wall. Before backfilling, perforated drain pipes are installed to channel any water filtering through the drain rock away from the wall. Filter fabric is also used to prevent the retained earth from clogging the drain rock and pipe.

45. **B** The minimum wall construction to meet ICBO requirements for 1-hour wall assemblies would be 2 × 4 wood studs at 24 inches on center with one layer of ⅝-in type X (fire-rated) gypsum wallboard attached to each side with specific nailing patterns. The other assemblies listed do not carry a 1-hour rating for their construction.

46. **C** The floor of a restaurant kitchen is subject to heavy traffic, exposure to water and constant cleaning, and requires a durable, waterproof installation. The only recommended method for installing ceramic tile over a concrete floor would be to set the tile in a full bed of cement mortar. The other methods of adhering ceramic tile would be appropriate only in areas not subject to such wear and exposure, such as decorative wall finishes or residential uses.

47. **D** A mortise lock would be the best choice for such a use. Mortise locks have the most operating functions available and are strong and durable, providing security and low maintenance. The next best choice would be cylindrical locks.

48. **A** High-rise buildings are required by building codes to have sprinkler systems and areas of refuge. Depending on the location used, interior finishes may be any one of the three classes. Only two stairways are required unless the occupant load of a floor and the floors above it is 500 or more.

49. **D** All public accommodations and commercial facilities, constructed after January 26, 1993, whether publicly or privately owned, are required by Title III of the Americans with Disabilities Act (ADA) to be accessible to the physically disabled. This includes site and parking lot access, entrances, corridors, exitways, elevators, toilet rooms, water fountains, telephones, etc., so as not to restrict access of the physically disabled to any occupied space (with few exceptions). To restrict access to areas used by the general public would discriminate against physically disabled employees (ADA Title I) and visitors alike. Various standards are delineated by the Americans with Disabilities Act, the Uniform Federal Accessibility Standards (UFAS), the American National Standards Institute (ANSI), the

Uniform Building Code, and other state and local regulations. These standards are intended for virtually all public and private buildings with only limited exemptions.

50. **C** Moisture content in dry lumber cannot exceed 19 percent. Design values for lumber used in structural engineering tables assume lumber with a moisture content not greater than 19 percent, otherwise the tabular values would have to be decreased. Kiln-dry lumber, as specified for the interior shelving, cannot have higher than 15 percent moisture content.

Suggested Reading

General Reference

American National Standards Institute. *Specifications for Making Buildings and Facilities Accessible to and Usable by Physically Handicapped People* (ANSI A117.1-1986). New York: American National Standards Institute, 1986.

Ballast, David Kent. *Architecture Exam Review*. Belmont, CA: Professional Publications, Inc., 1988.

Callender, John Hancock. *Time-Saver Standards for Architectural Design Data*. New York: McGraw-Hill, 1982.

DeChiara, Joseph, and John Hancock Callender. *Time-Saver Standards for Building Types*. New York: McGraw-Hill, 1982.

Goldberg, Alfred. *Design Guide to the Uniform Building Code*. Mill Valley, CA: GRDA Publications, 1991.

Haviland, David, ed. *Architect's Handbook of Professional Practice*. Washington, DC: American Institute of Architects, 1988.

International Conference of Building Officials. *Uniform Building Code*. Whittier, CA: International Conference of Building Officials, 1991.

National Council of Architectural Registration Boards. *Architect Registration Examination Handbook*. Washington, DC: National Council of Architectural Registration Boards, 1988.

National Fire Protection Association. *Life Safety Code*, NFPA No. 101. Quincy, MA: National Fire Protection Association, 1984.

Packard, Robert T., ed. *Architectural Graphic Standards*. New York: John Wiley & Sons, 1988.

U.S. Department of Justice, Office of the Attorney General. *Uniform Federal Accessibility Standards*. Canoga Park, CA: Builder's Book Inc., 1991.

Pre-Design

Bacon, Edmund N. *Design of Cities*. New York: Viking Press, 1976.

Fletcher, Sir Banister. *A History of Architecture on the Comparative Method*, 18th ed. New York: Macmillan, 1975.

Halprin, Lawrence. *Cities*. Van Nostrand Reinhold, New York: 1985.

Kratovil, Robert. *Real Estate Law*. Englewood Cliffs, NJ: Prentice-Hall, Inc., 1988.

McHarg, Ian. *Design with Nature*. New York: John Wiley & Sons, Inc., 1992.

Preiser, Wolfgang F. E. *Programming the Built Environment*. New York: Van Nostrand Reinhold, 1985.

Rasmussen, S. *Experiencing Architecture*. Cambridge, MA: MIT Press, 1992.

Structural Technology

American Concrete Institute. *Building Code Requirements for Reinforced Concrete*, ACI 318-89. Detroit: American Concrete Institute, 1989.

American Institute of Steel Construction. *Manual of Steel Construction*, 9th ed. Chicago: American Institute of Steel Construction, 1989.

American Institute of Timber Construction. *Timber Construction Manual*, 4th ed. Englewood, CO: John Wiley & Sons, 1993.

Parker, Harry. *Simplified Design of Reinforced Concrete*. New York: John Wiley & Sons, 1984.

_____ . *Simplified Design of Steel Structures*. New York: John Wiley & Sons, 1990.

_____ . *Simplified Engineering for Architects and Builders*. New York: John Wiley & Sons, 1989.

_____ . *Simplified Mechanics and Strength of Materials*. New York: John Wiley & Sons, 1992.

Salvadori, Mario, and Matthys Levy. *Structural Design in Architecture*, 2nd ed. Englewood Cliffs, NJ: Prentice-Hall, Inc., 1981.

Salvadori, Mario, and Robert Heller. *Structure in Architecture: The Building of Buildings*. Englewood Cliffs, NJ: Prentice-Hall, Inc., 1986.

Steel Joist Institute. *Standard Specifications for Steel Joists*. Myrtle Beach, SC: Steel Joist Institute.

Mechanical, Plumbing, Electrical, and Acoustical Systems

American Society of Heating, Refrigerating and Air Conditioning Engineers, Inc. *ASHRAE Handbook of Fundamentals*. Atlanta: American Society of Heating, Refrigerating and Air Conditioning Engineers, Inc., 1993.

Babbitt, Harold E. *Plumbing*. New York: McGraw-Hill, 1986.

Dagostino, Frank R. *Mechanical and Electrical Systems in Buildings*. Reston, VA: Reston Publishing Company, 1982.

Egan, M. David. *Architectural Acoustics*. New York: McGraw-Hill, 1988.

_____ . *Concepts in Lighting for Architecture*. New York: McGraw-Hill, 1983.

Illuminating Engineering Society of North America. *IES Lighting Handbook*. New York: Illuminating Engineering Society of North America, 1981.

International Conference of Building Officials. *Uniform Mechanical Code*. Whittier, CA: International Conference of Building Officials, 1991.

International Conference of Building Officials. *Uniform Plumbing Code*. Whittier, CA: International Conference of Building Officials, 1991.

Mazria, Edward. *The Passive Solar Energy Book*. Emmaus, PA: Rodale Press, Inc., 1979.

National Fire Protection Association. *National Electric Code*, NFPA 70. Quincy, MA: National Fire Protection Association, 1993.

Stein, Benjamin, John S. Reynolds and W.J. McGuinness. *Mechanical and Electrical Equipment for Buildings*, 8th ed. New York: John Wiley & Sons, 1992.

Materials and Methods

Architectural Woodwork Institute. *Architectural Woodwork Quality Standards, Guide Specifications and Quality Certifications Program*. Arlington, VA: Architectural Woodwork Institute, 1984.

Ellison, Donald C., Robert Mickadeit, and W. C. Huntington. *Building Construction, Materials and Types of Construction*. New York: John Wiley & Sons, 1987.

Harris, Cyril M. *Dictionary of Architecture and Construction*. New York: McGraw-Hill, 1987.

Prestressed Concrete Institute. *Precast/Prestressed Concrete Design Handbook*. Chicago: Prestressed Concrete Institute, 1985.

Randall, R. A., and W. C. Panarese. *Concrete Masonry Handbook*. Skokie, IL: Portland Cement Association, 1985.

Wakita, Osamu, and Richard M. Linde. *The Professional Handbook of Architectural Detailing*. New York: John Wiley & Sons, 1987.

Construction Documents and Services

Ballast, David Kent. *The Architect's Handbook*. Englewood Cliffs, NJ: Prentice-Hall, Inc., 1984.

Construction Inspection Manual. Los Angeles: BNI Books, 1990.

The Construction Specifications Institute. *Manual of Practice*. Alexandria, VA: The Construction Specifications Institute, 1985.

Greenstreet, Robert, and Karen Greenstreet. *The Architect's Guide to Law and Practice*. New York: Van Nostrand Reinhold, 1984.

Haviland, David S. *Managing Architectural Projects: The Process*. Washington, DC: The American Institute of Architects Service Corp., 1981.

Mahoney, William D., editor-in-chief. *Building Construction Cost Data.* Kingston, MA: R.S. Means Company, Inc., 1994.

Nigro, William T. *Redicheck Interdisciplinary Coordination.* Stone Mountain, GA: The Redicheck Firm, 1987.

Rosen, Harold. *Construction Specifications Writing: Principles and Procedures.* New York: John Wiley & Sons, Inc., 1981.

Saylor, Leland S. *Current Construction Costs.* Concord, CA: Saylor Publications, Inc., 1996 (published yearly).

Superintendent of Documents. *Occupational Safety and Health Act of 1970.* Washington, DC: U.S. Government Printing Office, 1993.

About the Author

Larry A. Paul, AIA, received his formal education at Ohio State University and the University of Southern California and was awarded the Bachelor of Architecture professional degree in 1970. He was first licensed in 1974, having passed the entire ARE the first time he took it.

Mr. Paul has practiced as principal in his own architectural and planning firm since 1976. His experience has included an extensive range of project types and sizes, with responsibilities in all phases of architectural services for a variety of clients.

Mr. Paul is a member of the American Institute of Architects (AIA) and is licensed in California and Hawaii.

He also holds a certificate with the National Council of Architectural Registration Boards (NCARB), the organization that administers the ARE. He has served as a Design Juror for the NCARB ARE Building and Site Design Exam and the California Architectural Licensing Exam (CALE).

As a part of his commitment to serving his community, Mr. Paul has been a member of several local design review boards. In addition, he is a Master Commissioner on the California Board of Architectural Examiners (CBAE) and a member of the Orals and Internship Committee. CBAE develops and administers the Oral Exam given to candidates for licensing in California as a final supplement to the ARE.